So You're Going To Have A Baby?

Your Guide to Navigating Medical Decisions Before, During, and After Pregnancy

Preface

I'd like to dedicate this book to our pediatrician who is one of the most caring and wonderful doctors I've ever met. In an insane world of medical abominations – there stands at least one who actually listens to his patients and finds the answers to their questions. While we may not agree on everything – I respect him greatly and am so grateful that he took us on as patients during my wife's pregnancy.

At our last "well baby checkup" I told him that I would attempt to write this book as if I were visiting with him – respectfully, compassionately, and like another human being.

My wife and I had a difficult time finding a pediatrician that would take us on. We're a bit on the hippie side (OK maybe a lot on the hippie side). We actually didn't go into the hospital after we found out we were pregnant until probably 22 weeks – we just didn't feel the need to. She was pregnant – no doubt about that – and we weren't having anything that would raise any alarms that we would need to go in to have a checkup – we were just doing as people have done for however long they've been around – having a baby. As our good doctor says – he really doesn't do anything but let nature do its thing unless something goes wrong. So that's what we were doing – just enjoying my wife's pregnancy.

The first doctor we went to was a bit of a nightmare to deal with – she actually had us barred from the entire hospital because we didn't want to do an unnecessary ultrasound on the baby (I will describe why we made this decision later). It was have an ultrasound "because she said so" – or she wouldn't see us. As it turned out – it meant the entire hospital wouldn't see us. But I digress – it's just an example of why we chose to find a doctor like our current one – who would listen to why we were making the decision we were.

The first doctor actually had a drug test ordered because we didn't come in right away when we were pregnant. I suppose I could see her reasoning – most people rush right in as if something is wrong the second they know they're pregnant. That's what this book is for – to approach the stigma that being pregnant is somehow a disease that needs to be treated – instead of something that has been happening since the beginning of the creation of life – a gift.

I'm not saying don't go to your doctor if you need to – I'm just saying maybe don't go until you need to (or the appropriate time arrives). Hospitals ARE filled with MRSA and other infectious diseases – after all it's not where you go to find healthy people. Your greatest chance of catching one of the more resistant diseases is at a hospital – so the less unnecessary trips the better. I mean – it IS where sick people go – not healthy people. That's all I'm saying.

Of course being me – I did go back to the hospital that banned us and brought in over 80 studies – all highlighted at major talking points and concerns for their convenience – on our reasoning not to get an ultrasound that we didn't need. Alas – their decision stood. I suppose, however – it was a blessing. Had we stayed there – we wouldn't have the awesome doctor we do now. Also I probably wouldn't be writing this book. Perspective, I suppose.

The reason we didn't want an ultrasound – wasn't because we thought we knew better than the doctors there. It's just

3

because we had questions – ones that they not only didn't have the answer to, but wouldn't even entertain.

To put another piece of information out there for you to help inform you on why our family has the stance is does – is this link:
https://draxe.com/conventional-medicine-is-the-leading-cause-of-death/

It's not only this link that will tell you this – but many irrefutable studies. Basically – conventional medicine kills MORE people than cancer or heart disease ever year.

It's the equivalent of 6 jumbo jets per day falling out of the sky – every single day.

I don't know about anyone else – but I'm more concerned with those numbers of deaths – than I am deaths from say Measles. There has been possible only **ONE** in the last 10 years – and that person also had multiple other coinfections. I'm just saying logically by the numbers – the less you have to go in for any form of medical procedures/interventions that aren't really necessary – the better. That isn't my opinion – it's numbers.

I share this story because there are both good and bad doctors. There are doctors who "treat a chart" – and doctors who treat patients. Try to find one that does the latter – because no two circumstances are the same (unless of course you're going to vote – you're going to get screwed every time no matter who you vote for).

A special thanks to my co-author Chris Kirckof for his passion and dedication to finding all the resources I needed to put this together in a logical fashion. I had at one point looked almost all of them up – but didn't keep record of it. His diligence and dedication to this book and to his family are extremely appreciated. It wouldn't be here if not for his help.

To clarify – this book is not an anti-vaccine or anti-medical procedure book by any means. There are times that medical intervention is the best option.

This book is an attempt to help you not only have all the information to back up your decisions on why you make your choice – but far more importantly – the questions to ask. Answers are never important unless you know the right question to ask – because the answer changes depending upon the question. So if you only want the answer – you're only getting half the picture. Something I will admit the pharmaceutical industry is good at – astroturfing half the issue – and pretending the other side doesn't exist and isn't important. Once again this is not your doctor. This is, in reality, OUR fault – because we stopped asking questions – and wanted everyone to do the work for us.

So as you go about making decisions – make sure it is not because you think this book TOLD you to. That is the exact opposite of what this book is for. This book is to arm you with information to help you make the right decision for yourself – and to ask the right questions.

A child will potentially – and hopefully – be the most important person in your life. I urge you to spend as much time researching every questions, medical procedure, and answer to the questions – as you would researching your next cell phone, your next car, your next house, computer, sports ticket, kitchen appliance, you get the idea. Involve yourself in the entire process – don't just let someone else tell you what to do.

Also – be aware that if you are going to Google something – pharmaceutical companies have skewed the results in many, many cases. They astroturf, publish fake or duplicate articles, have algorithms run searches and clicks, basically have made it so anything that doesn't fit their narrative gets buried on page 100.

Well – go to search page 100 until you find both sides of an argument.

If anyone tells you that you shouldn't look at the other side of things – that is a sure sign that you should do just the opposite – because there's probably something to hide.

There is no "right" answer when it comes to you and your baby's medical decision – only what's right for YOU. Spend more time looking into your questions than you do watching *Game of Thrones* or whatever other show there is to binge watch.

Granted – I agree it might be more fun to binge watch – it is far more expensive than just the time you spent on the couch. There's all the decisions that you had somebody else make for you – that is another cost.

As a final note – I would like to point out that this book is **NOT** an anti-medical procedure or anti-vaccine book – it is more an "other side of the story" book. The benefits of the medical system are well known – the shortcomings not so much. So while I may point out most of the reasons not to use medical interventions – I point them out only because they aren't very well known. Please try to keep that in mind – that I'm just trying to make sure the other side of the story comes out.

Your doctor is an incredible wealth of knowledge, try your best to have an open discussion with him or her – because no one person knows everything.

If we can work together – we can help make the best decisions for everyone – and especially our children.

In the end – there is no greater mistake than to put the decisions regarding you or your family's health solely into the hands of someone who bears none of the consequences.

Table of Contents

Chapter 1

Pre-Pregnancy

In this chapter we're going to address a few issues that hopefully can not only help you conceive, but make the process easier as well. One of the crucial things to understand is that if your body isn't healthy enough to have a baby – it's not going to have one. If it's barely hanging on trying to support you – it's not going to add an additional stressor to the load it already has. Many people opt straight for hormone therapy to attempt to conceive – which I stress you should really think about first. The link to cancers later in women who have done this is one that should highly be considered – especially when there are other options.

Detoxification

Anyone who is planning to become pregnant or have a child should certainly entertain attempting to reduce their toxicity load. A person should really start a year (or even two) before wanting to become pregnant – because in most circumstances doing a detox while pregnant is a really bad idea (also most people don't know how to properly do a detox – no fault of their own – but it's not an easy thing to do – and each detox and person is different).

It's that "ounce of prevention – pound of cure" thing.

The detoxes mentioned in this chapter should be performed 12 months before trying to get pregnant. Doing a "detox" while pregnant is in nearly every circumstance a VERY bad idea.

Had to make that part really, really clear. Plan ahead – your family will thank you.

One of the largest things to avoid and detoxify are what are called "**XenoEstrogens**" – molecules that act like hormones in the human body but are 100-1000x times more powerful than your own hormones. These include things like fragrances from plug-in air fresheners, dryer sheets/fabric softeners, and other synthetic fragrances.

I'm not going to go super in depth here as it's very easy to locate information on this topic and I encourage the reader to look into it.

I WILL however say – these can disrupt your ability to become pregnant. If you're putting it on every day – over time this adds up. This can greatly interfere with your body's ability to produce enough hormones, like progesterone, that are needed to sustain a pregnancy.

RoundUp –

The propensity for RoundUp to disrupt hormones is something I can't stress enough. Same topic as with the XenoEstrogens – this one really starts to add up – fast.

Take a look into how modern wheat is doused with weed-killer right before it is harvested to increase yields. As a final death knell to continue its generations on – the wheat in response to poison does all it can to make a seed that can possibly survive.

Do a little Google search on the levels of RoundUp found in Cheerios and Triscuits – you'll see the levels are insane. No wonder everyone is "allergic to wheat".

RoundUp can disrupt your hormones so incredibly that it makes getting pregnant nearly impossible.

Finally on the RoundUp subject – independent researchers recently held a congressional hearing on the RoundUp being found in many different vaccines. I personally called the FDA and asked about it – they were well aware of the test results and contamination – but had no plans to test any vaccines at all to ensure they were free from contamination. I don't know about you – but that's not exactly a response that I feel confident in agreeing with. No one has any idea what the safe level of injectable weed-killer into children is – those tests have never been done. The fact that the FDA told me they were aware of it but planned to do absolutely nothing only solidifies my opinion of them further.

Also, in the same congressional hearing – a good friend of mine Sterling Hill (brilliant, brilliant lady) mapped out and showed the synthetic amino acid in RoundUp is replacing the natural amino acid in our DNA and disabling detoxification and causing the MTHFR epigenetic epidemic we have today (more on this later). Of course – two weeks after the hearing – the D.A.R.K. Act (Deny Americans the Right to Know) was passed by Congress and the whole topic was shut down – and Monsanto was given extra congressional favors and protection. Pretty neat, huh? Hate to break it to you – but the fastest way to destroy you and your family's genetics is to consume any Monsanto products. This includes GMO – sorry. Anyone that tells you otherwise either has no idea what they are talking about or is lying. Ask them about horizontal gene transfer in gram-positive promiscuous bacteria from the altered DNA in GMOs. If their eyes glaze over – rest assured you don't want to listen to their opinion on GMOs that has been astroturfed into their brain by the same companies that sell GMOs. GMOs have nothing to do with "feeding the world" – but we will shelf that topic again for another day. Also – GMOs are usually sprayed with more RoundUp than non-GMO products. That reason right there should be enough to avoid them like the plagues they are.

Also – I know this is a not a medical journal – but the information here is of utmost importance and ask that you read it over: https://foodbabe.com/2016/11/15/monsanto/

Mercury Fillings

Your dentist might call them "amalgam" – but they are mercury. Feel free to look up the documentary called "Smoking Teeth" on YouTube to get a picture of the danger they pose. Also – ask your dentist to bring out the container marked "Biohazard" that he pulls the stuff from they claim it's safe. Proof is in the pudding, as they say.

Also, recent studies have found that WiFi and cell phones cause them to leach mercury into the body over twice as fast as without it. If you get them removed – be sure it's at a holistic dentist where they use the proper ventilation and dams to block the toxins released during their removal. This is also advised to be done a year ahead of time if possible – as some mercury will still leach into the body even with all of the proper precautions.**Fluoride**

Avoiding fluoride at all costs is a large priority as well. Your dentist will tell you that you need fluoride to have healthy teeth – keep in mind these are the same people shoving mercury in your mouth. Just a little perspective.

Bottom line is – fluoride is a neurotoxin. Plain and simple. It is not something that just comes out of the ground like a natural mineral – it is hazardous industrial waste that comes from scrubbers in the smoke stacks of the aluminum and phosphate (and nuclear) industries. It's too toxic to be put into the air, groundwater, or rivers – so they have to remove it via EPA standards.

The funny part is – they used to have to pay to dispose of it until someone "tobacco science'd" up a study in which a town with naturally occurring fluoride had lower incidence of tooth decay. I'm just going to let this following chart on the largest study of fluoride and tooth decay ever done do the talking:

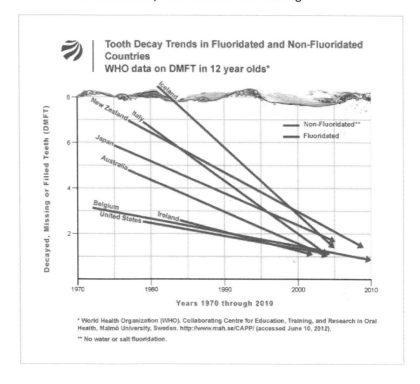

As you can see – countries with and without fluoridated water are at nearly identical tooth decay rates – putting a really big "cavity" in the whole "we need fluoride for our teeth" propaganda.

On top of this – Harvard has recently lumped fluoride into the same category as lead, arsenic, and mercury – completely toxic in any and all amounts. It's not just the fluoride that's an issue either – the fluoride combines with heavy metals to make it infinitely more toxic than it would be without it. A simple

Google search on the dangers of fluoride will yield all the research you should need – and we will be archiving it all on the website we are creating to give people access to all the files and data we collect and mention.

Fluoride also interferes with the ability of the umbilical cord to attach to the uterine wall – because it interferes with the body's ability to make collagen. Without this collagen the umbilical cord can't form properly with the uterine wall. Also – collagen is what helps keep skin healthy – so avoiding fluoride can do wonders for your skin.

On a final note – fluoride is not only neurotoxic, it is also nephrotoxic (kidneys), hepatotoxic (liver), along with basically every other single body part you can name. Dental fluorosis is also a large problem today – due to kids consuming too much fluoride. Remember that no long-term (or even short-term) studies have been done on fluoride except for levels of dental fluorosis. Not exactly "sound science" – especially when they found that 41% of children (and this figure includes those in non-fluoridated areas – skewing the data) have dental fluorosis – a sign that a person has ingested too much fluoride. Well – if it damages the teeth (actually making them more susceptible to cavities) – and there's hundreds of studies on its toxicity to other body parts – reason would stand that other organs have been damaged as well in some way, shape, or form. Conveniently, however, this has never been studied. You'll find that trend seems to happen a lot throughout the course of this book.

Fluoride is also a widely used insecticide. As a final nail in the coffin…

Fluoride is so toxic that you as an individual could not buy it if you wanted to. It is the active ingredient in Sarin nerve gas. If you spill it – it will eat holes in concrete. That's why you can't

14

buy it.

So if you still want to consume it – well – at this point I probably can't say anything to stop you.

Except maybe that it displaces iodine in the body – which is used by the thyroid to regulate metabolism (in case you were wondering why there are so many thyroid issues in America – here is part of why). Also mothers with lower iodine levels are at greater risk for kids with autism. I could go on for an entire book on this topic alone – but let's just leave it at this for now.

This one link from the FDA should sum up partially the concerns with the neurotoxin fluoride:
https://www.fda.gov/ohrms/dockets/dockets/07p0070/07p-0070-cp00001-02-vol1.pdf
This article will be of great importance when I get to the topic of aluminum – so be sure to keep it handy or at least note that *fluoride drastically increases the toxicity of all other heavy metals*.

Probiotics

Probiotics are a DEFINITE help – and starting early is even better. Your body takes a while to adopt the beneficial microorganisms that have been killed off by the chlorine in our water supply, antibiotics, the standard American diet full of glyphosate (RoundUp), the whole works.

A baby inherits its entire microbiome from its mother – so if your gut health is off – it puts the baby at risk for many different issues down the road. Up to 70% or more of the immune system is actually located in the gut, and up to 70% of neurotransmitters are made there as well (as well as vitamin and mineral assimilation).

My favorite probiotic is one called EM-1 from www.freshandalive.com. It's called a "soil conditioner" – kind of like "raw milk is for pets" if you get the idea. I use that stuff to brew gallons of my own probiotics for pennies on the dollar. Our whole family uses it, and we put some in our essential oil diffuser in the winter or any time we need to help boost our immune systems and let it diffuse in the house. You can also use the stuff to clean up mold – and is being used to clean up radioactive material around Fukushima (let's not even get started on that topic). Long story short – this stuff is awesome and will save you a fortune on probiotics.

Iodine

Iodine is a nutrient that is one of the strongest killers of fungus, bacterial, parasites, and cancer in the world. There's a reason they sterilize wounds with it in hospitals – it's amazing against infections. The reason I mention it here is not for the infections so much (however it doesn't hurt for that) but for bone and thyroid health. I mentioned briefly about how fluoride lowers iodine levels in the body – so if you've been on city water your whole life – I would put this at the top of your list.

Iodine also helps displace heavy metals and things like bromine from the body. Those up on the topic of geoengineering will understand why this is doubly important.

My favorite kind is Dr. Cousen's "Illumodine" – a very special form of ultra-bioavailable iodine. You can get it https://www.drcousensonlinestore.com/?Click=17759 and search for "**Illumodine**" as of now.

What makes this iodine so special is multifaceted. Instead of being an ionic form like potassium iodide or sodium iodide – this iodine is completely pure without a "memory" of where it has been before. It is also "monoatomic" – meaning it's not two atoms of iodine attached together (diatomic) and it has been broken down into an angstrom size (basically – very small). Think of it this way:

Clusters of an element come in "popcorn balls" – basically there's a bunch of atoms or molecules in a lump of whatever size the particle is broken down to. Now, this lump isn't exactly very well used by the body in a lot of circumstances. It's like you trying to eat a two-foot popcorn ball – not going to happen until you break it down to smaller pieces you can fit in your mouth. I had a grandma that had very tough popcorn balls I used to have to break with nothing short of a hammer. Probably because she left them out for god knows how long. The point of the story is that this iodine is already broken down into super small "popcorn balls" so your body can use it readily instead of having to exert energy to "break the ball apart".

Like I said – very multifaceted reasons why it's a great product – there's more – but let's just use these simple examples for the sake of the book's length.

Cell Phones/WiFi

Like I've said in other books of mine – the more you can avoid these the better. Cell phones – there's a reason they call them "cell phones" – because they are damaging to cells and DNA (or so I'm told). Think of all the damage that can be caused by having one of (especially the new ones) these phones in your pocket all day, men, next to your testicles. Let's not get too far into what that really does – besides it's a bad, bad thing. Cell phones and WiFi also will cause the mercury fillings in your mouth to release twice as much mercury per day into the body when exposed to them. So those living next to a cell phone tower – you might want to think about that.

While it's nearly impossible to avoid the electromagnetic soup we live in – we can take precautions to avoid the exposure. Make sure the WiFi is not near a room that you or your kids are sleeping in – and DO NOT charge your phone at night next to your head or leave it near you while you sleep. Worst idea ever. Also – it's completely free to just move it across the room. So the cheapest thing you can do is just make sure that your WiFi and cell phones are not near you or your kids while you sleep.

Those of you with the cojones to really look stuff up – look up a guy named "Barrie Trower" on YouTube and hear what he's got to say about the death towers, smart (death) meters, and silly phones all around us. Expect it to take a little bit to sink in.

Microwaves (cell signals) and WiFi also interact with heavy metals – trapping them in the body. So you're going to have a hard time excreting them if they are trapped in the body by electromagnetic radiation. They also interact violently with microwaves (put tinfoil in the microwave and you'll see) – and since these metals have an affinity for the brain and nerves – anything you can do to avoid or limit your exposure the better. There are many researchers that argue that this electromagnetic smog and the metal adjuvants in vaccines are greatly contributing to autism – however this author feels it is only a piece of the puzzle.

A big enough piece however to warrant this writer to not sleep with his phone by him and shut off the WiFi at night even though it's across the house.

Side note – iPads and other tablet devices also should be kept away from pregnant women and kids as much as possible. I get it though – tough to do these days. Do your best.

MTHFR and Folic Acid

I'll approach MTHFR a little later in the book (because it is **very** important) but I'd like to stick to the topic of nutrition pre-pregnancy right now.

The problem we have these days is we live in a world of "synthetic nutrition" – produced by people who honestly have nearly zero idea how nutrition actually works.

I'll put this really simply – a synthetic vitamin will **never** be the same as a natural one. We can't put the same electron spins and lord only knows what subatomic properties are present that we just aren't aware of – and to think otherwise would be completely idiotic.

Take folic acid for example –

Folic acid is the synthetic version of folate – more specifically methylfolate. Methylfolate is the actual usable version in the body – folic acid is actually poisonous.

When you take folic acid – your body has to go through a dozen metabolic steps to convert it to its usable version. Until it has been fully converted – your body can't do anything with it and even worse it's toxic.

Remember how every doctor (and even TV shows like "Orange is the New Black") said to take your folic acid while pregnant?

Yeah – worst idea ever. OK maybe not ever – but it's a really bad idea.

Specifically why – is there (thanks to RoundUp) are increasingly more people who genetically don't have the ability to methylate things in the body and produce detoxification enzymes.

Remember how I said the useable form of folic acid was **methyl**folate? That's right – so those with that genetic deficiency cannot efficiently convert the poison known as folic acid into the usable form. What this leads to is elevated levels

19

of the unusable form of folic acid free floating in the blood. The body (and the fetus) will respond by shutting off receptors to both methylfolate AND folic acid at the same time – because there is too much of the toxic version floating around.

Essentially what the cells do is "shut the gates" to the excess levels of a poisonous substance – effectively at the same time locking out the usable form. You can find loads of research on why folate is important for healthy fetal development if you look (or ask your doctor) – there isn't room for all the reasons here.

Your solution is to juice spinach (where it is naturally found in high levels) or get a good, organic, whole-food vitamin supplement.

The same thing also applies the vitamin **CyanoCobalamin** – the synthetic version of vitamin B12 (methylcobalamin). This one is even worse – because the part of the vitamin your body needs to methylate is attached to a cyanide molecule. So when your body breaks down the only thing available to make an essential vitamin – it poisons you. A double whammy. This vitamin is also found in extreme quantities in many energy drinks and crap vitamins because it's CHEAP – and the rocket scientists at the FDA do not know the difference between the two. According to them the cyanide is "safely excreted" – of course with no explanation on how exactly cyanide is made "safe".

Long story short – the rhetoric that a synthetic vitamin is the same as natural – is a story only those who have no idea what they're talking about tell.

So do yourself a favor and avoid synthetic vitamins (and help educate people on how they are not the same – a copy of this book always works well...).

Granted – not exactly their fault. Once again "science" has been swayed by monetary interests to make sure people don't know about the difference (this includes government regulatory agencies – sorry).

Heavy Metals

Under almost all circumstances – a heavy metal detox is going to be extremely hard. I have however found a product that makes it MUCH easier that I will talk about toward the end of the book – because it solves nearly all of the problems with standard heavy metal detoxes or chelation therapies.

If you are going to attempt a heavy metal detox (unless using the product from the end of the book) **do not do it within 3 months of attempting to get pregnant.**

Nearly all forms of heavy metal detox regimens don't work all that well. You have to cycle supplements, eating, nutrients, foods, it's honestly just an extreme amount of work and you really need to know what you're doing.

So do yourself a favor – either use the Coseva TRS mentioned at the end of the book – or get professional help on how to do it correctly. I can't stress this enough.

Your best bet is to limit exposure to heavy metals in makeup, fluoridated products, GMO foods, mercury fillings, and as I will talk about – vaccines.

Chapter 2

Pregnancy

Folic Acid

I mentioned this earlier in the book – simply refer to that spot on why to avoid this.

Ultrasounds

As I mentioned in the preface of this book, usually the first thing that happens as soon as someone is pregnant is they go in and get their ultrasound.

I would like to be clear – I am not "anti-ultrasound" – I am merely here to inform you that there are risks involved with them. Every medical procedure has risks, and many of them aren't well known – even to people in the medical field. Of course if you need one – get one – however in the next little bit I'll attempt to explain why it should only be if you need one.

The first misconception is that the baby can't hear the ultrasound. The ultrasounds used are about 110 decibels – which is the equivalent of a subway train coming into a station – and by 18 weeks the baby can certainly hear it. Think of the highest note on a piano being hit to the volume of a subway train coming into the station – for up to 30 minutes straight. This is an ultrasound for the baby.

In the late 90s to early 2000s the FDA raised the volume limits on ultrasounds by 8 times without conducting any safety studies whatsoever. The problem with this is multiple-fold.

Keep in mind that just because everyone is doing something or is universally medically recommended – doesn't mean it's the right thing to do. We used to x-ray every pregnant woman, and used to put screws into the fetus's head to monitor heartbeats. Sure we know better now – but at the time they thought they knew better too. This is just a side food for thought. I'm not saying it's the same – but I am saying raising the volume level by 8 times without thinking about it might not be a good idea.

Ultrasounds can also be used to separate the blood-brain barrier, deliver drugs across the blood-brain barrier, and alter brainwaves and mental states. Do a Google search on any of these topics – they are very easy to find.

So here becomes the problem. Are you on any medications? If so – opening the blood-brain barrier and possibly forcing these across that barrier with ultrasounds might not be a good idea for the baby. Heavy metals? Those can be pushed across as well. The DTaP vaccine and the flu vaccine (despite never once being studied for safety) are routinely recommended for all pregnant women (once again despite absolutely no safety studies). Ultrasounds can drastically increase the risk of heavy metals (adjuvants) being pushed across the blood-brain barrier. Also these heavy metals respond to ultrasound frequencies – by heating up.

Now, you don't have to be a rocket scientist to figure out that pushing heavy metals across the blood-brain barrier and then having ultrasonic waves heat them up – might not be the best idea in the world. If your doctor recommends a vaccine while pregnant and then wants to send you in for an ultrasound – I would immediately find a new doctor who has some form of common sense. You can ask them what data they used to support such procedures and why they can justify such a dangerous practice – but the thing is no studies at all exist even partly. So unless he or she can hand you the studies showing the safety of doing it and not doing It – I wouldn't believe much they have to say. Both of the vaccine inserts currently state in clear wording "this vaccine has not been studied for safety in pregnant women". You can decide if you want to put your child up for a medical experiment if you want – my wife and I however opted out of that experiment.

There is also localized heating that occurs – which can be up to a 4-degree Celsius rise in temperature. This is about 7.2 degrees Fahrenheit. Think of it this way – if your child got a fever of 7.2 degrees above normal (almost 106 degrees) – you'd probably be headed to the hospital with that child. Granted – this is not an overall rise in temperature – it is not the same thing – however it is worth thinking about if raising temperatures in the brain that much would be something you want to do or not.

There is also something called "mechanical shearing" that happens when the amniotic fluid in the womb responds to the energy waves propagating through it – causing the cells and neurons to adopt different cymatic patterns. Look up the topic of "cymatics" (Nigel Stanford has an amazing music video on this) to get a clear picture of what happens. The argument some doctors and scientists make is that we honestly have no idea what that does to a brain – especially for prolonged exposure like a 30-minute routine ultrasound.

Another concern is something called "cavitation" – where due to pressure changes an air bubble will form in the water and then rapidly collapse upon itself raising the temperature incredibly (I mean really incredibly) for a short period of time. This can also result in something called "sonoluminescence" where the collapse of the air bubble causes light to spontaneously be released from the air bubble (no one really knows why).

Here's a quote from Wikipedia (yes I know – Wikipedia is a very, very poor source to site – however in this circumstance I find it acceptable):

Cavitation is the formation of vapour cavities in a liquid – i.e. small liquid-free zones ("bubbles" or "voids") – that are the consequence of forces acting upon the liquid. It usually occurs when a liquid is subjected to rapid changes of <u>pressure</u> that cause the formation of cavities in the liquid where the pressure is relatively low. When subjected to higher pressure, the voids implode and can generate an intense shock wave.

Cavitation is a significant cause of wear in some engineering contexts. Collapsing voids that implode near to a metal surface cause cyclic stress through repeated implosion. This results in surface fatigue of the metal causing a type of wear also called "cavitation". The most common examples of this kind of wear are to pump impellers, and bends where a sudden change in the direction of liquid occurs. Cavitation is usually divided into two classes of behavior: inertial (or transient) cavitation and non-inertial cavitation.

Inertial cavitation is the process where a void or bubble in a liquid rapidly collapses, producing a shock wave. Inertial cavitation occurs in nature in the strikes of mantis shrimps and pistol shrimps, as well as in the vascular tissues of plants. In man-made objects, it can occur in control valves, pumps, propellers and impellers.

Non-inertial cavitation is the process in which a bubble in a fluid is forced to oscillate in size or shape due to some form of energy input, such as an acoustic field. Such cavitation is often employed in ultrasonic cleaning baths and can also be observed in pumps, propellers, etc.

Since the shock waves formed by collapse of the voids are strong enough to cause significant damage to moving parts, cavitation is usually an undesirable phenomenon. It is very often specifically avoided in the design of machines such as turbines or propellers, and eliminating cavitation is a major field in the study of fluid dynamics. However, it is sometimes useful and does not cause damage when the bubbles collapse away from machinery, such as in supercavitation.

So to sum it up – the process of cavitation can destroy metal propellers and is specifically engineered against to avoid it due to the damage it can cause. To what extent this happens with an ultrasound, there is no documentation or data on at this point that I have been able to find – so I will leave it up to you to decide how important it is to you.

Finally – ultrasounds can be given to male animals or people and it can cause them to be sterilized for 6 months or longer. You may easily find this information online as well – and decide for yourself just what effect exactly this might have on your unborn child – especially if it is male.

This information is not to scare you away from getting necessary ultrasounds – it is simply to let you be aware of the possible implications that should be considered when making a decision.

What I used to make my decision – was thinking of it this way:

Would I want to possibly be made high out of my mind on ultrasonic waves while listening to the highest note on the piano being played for 30 minutes at 110 decibels while possibly shuttling heavy metals or medications across the brain and mechanically deforming unknown areas of the body while inside of a sensory deprivation tank while locally heating unknown areas of the body to unknown temperatures? My answer to that was no – and I'm a full-grown adult. I have no idea what that does to a child who can't even breathe yet as far as experiences go.

Once again – not trying to scare you away from ultrasounds – just trying to paint a picture of things that should be considered.

Finally, many hospitals will use "breech" (where the baby is feet first) as a justification for every person needing an ultrasound – but here's the thing:

The majority of these correct themselves on their own eventually – and if the baby is like that – there is nothing the doctor can do. So my thinking point would be – even if the baby WAS feet first at say 4 months of pregnancy – if it most likely will right itself – and there's nothing the hospital can do until the time of birth – what does it matter until right before birth? Finding out at 4 months isn't going to help anything – because by 6 or 7 months of pregnancy any good doctor should be able to tell if your baby is face down or feet down without an ultrasound.

If you absolutely still need one in case of breech – you could wait until the 8-month mark (or honestly even while in labor) to find out if your doctor couldn't tell – because until the birth time – it doesn't matter anyway.

Now of course as well they have these fancy new 4D ultrasounds that complicate matters even further. I don't have any opinion on them or research to state – because frankly there really isn't any – besides the FDA has advised to skip them if you can. Yes the "keepsake" of a picture of your baby in the womb is cool – but what cost are you really paying?

Also worth reading:
UK study found that healthy mothers and babies who received two or more doppler scans to check the placenta had more than 2 times the risk of perinatal death compared to babies unexposed to doppler.
https://www.ncbi.nlm.nih.gov/pubmed/1360032

Ultrasound: Weighing the Propaganda Against the Facts (While not a medical journal – it does indeed paint interesting arguments and have wonderful citations and links)
http://www.midwiferytoday.com/articles/ultrasound.asp

Other studies (from the 90's, when the ultrasounds were 7 times weaker) showed increased risk of miscarriage or preterm birth. One study included over 9,000 pregnant women in two

groups, one which received a routine ultrasound at 16-20 weeks and one group who didn't. In the group who received an ultrasound at 16-20 weeks, there were 16 fetal death after the 16-20 week period while there were none in the group who did not receive ultrasounds
https://www.ncbi.nlm.nih.gov/pubmed/22902073

Ultrasounds have not been shown to improve infant outcomes but may be increasing the rate of interventions used in pregnancies. One study found that knowledge of estimated fetal weight independently increased a woman's risk of having a c-section, yet fetal outcomes were not improved. That means OBs may be choosing to go ahead with c-sections based on fetal size alone, even when everything else is perfectly normal. https://www.ncbi.nlm.nih.gov/pubmed/22902073

All thoughts to keep in mind when you make the decision that is right for you.

Vaccination While Pregnant

If your doctor offers you one (or two) while pregnant – kindly ask them to pull out the vaccine insert and find the spots where it says "this product has never been studied for mutagenic or carcinogenic properties" and "this product has never been tested on pregnant women". Ask your doctor what reasoning or guarantee they have that it is safe when there are no studies to prove it.

If your doctor comes up with an answer that is satisfactory to you – obviously it is your decision. I personally take "because the CDC said so" despite no proof of safety – as them saying "time to find a new doctor".

No doctor should ever recommend a product that hasn't been tested for safety in pregnant women – to a pregnant woman. If you're going to be part of a medical experiment you should be getting paid. I'm not anti-vaccine – I'm pro-science. Prove it's safe, please.

Glucose (Blood Sugar) Test

I don't normally do this – but I'm just going to give you an article someone else has already written in a great format to go visit:

https://wellnessmama.com/77012/pregnancy-glucose-test/

She hits all the great talking points, and this is in my opinion just better to have you go read what she did vs. having me type up a very long segment here that I didn't actually do. My wife and I just declined the test because we have no indications that she is at risk for failing this. Also in the grand scheme of things – there are a lot more important topics to touch on than this one. Yes it's a sugary drink – but certainly not the end of the world. Not worth dwelling on much – just go check out her info if you feel you need to.

RoundUp and XenoExstrogens

I talked about this topic earlier – and the same applies here. Avoid them at all costs, as they can contribute to premature births or more difficult labor and C-sections.

Rhogam

This is a very tricky topic, so I'll do my best.

Rhogam is an injection that is given when the Rh factors in the blood and the baby don't match. If the blood from an Rh positive baby and an Rh negative mother mix, the mother can become "sensitized" to this. This basically means that if the mother were to have another Rh positive baby, there is a chance that the mother's immune system might not be very nice to that next baby. It can in some cases cause the death of the child.

29

However, on average it is estimated that only 10% of Rh negative women will become sensitized during their first pregnancy and childbirth. So that means – even if your Rh factors don't match – there is only a 10% chance that your blood will mix and potentially cause any problems. In those 10% of women, there is roughly a 1 in 4,000 chance that a future baby will be lost. I'm not saying there aren't risks in choosing not to get the shot, I'm just pointing out what they are in terms of numbers.

Now, onto the other part of it.

There have only been **9** studies done on Rhogam so far – all of them conducted in the 60s and 70s (half a century ago). Of them:

We don't know who paid for 7 of the 9 of them.

Only 2 of the 9 were double blind.

6 of the 9 were not random or were only quasi-random.

So that's all of the studies that have been done it. Here's the next part that troubled me when that time came – no studies have been done on either the parent or the child in terms of long-term health after the shot. That bothered me. Knowing that you're altering a part of the immune system and the way it will react to babies – for an undetermined period of time (honestly) – that no one has done any follow-up studies on.

Normally this used to be done with only parents who had blood types that could create a baby that was positive – or if there was suspicion of "unfaithfulness". Now, however – they just give it to everyone regardless. I asked my doctor (even though I knew the answer) and he kindly looked into if it was necessary for us – which it wasn't.

So to me – any time something is universally done without any thought to it whatsoever – that throws up huge red flags. This begs the question now because – if there WERE problems related to the Rhogam shot – you have eliminated any control group whatsoever. Now I, being the mind that I am, have a blatant distrust for pharmaceutical companies (rightfully so unfortunately). So in my mind, if I had a product that was causing harm – how could I cover it up so no one ever noticed? Well – just give it to everyone so there is no control group. I'm not saying that's happening, but I am saying the thought crossed my mind and affected my decision. Doesn't have to affect yours. I'm just pointing out that no one has bothered to do any follow up on the long-term ramifications of this product for some reason.

Next – the product does still contain Thimerosal. While it might say "mercury free" – what this means is that they filtered out as much as they could and got it to a level low enough they didn't have to report that mercury was still in it. Your doctor might not agree that Thimerosal is mercury – however the **hundreds** of studies we reference later in the book documenting its toxicity (as opposed to the CDC's 4 they use) might have you disagreeing with your doctor as well. Or something called the "Simpsonwood Meetings". Have fun with that one – don't say I didn't warn you.

The next thing is – no one knows what the optimal dose is. The United States gives 3 times as much as many other countries – and there are no studies on what giving different amounts does.

Another problem is – in some women the exact opposite of what is supposed to happen happens. In some women the shot actually makes the woman's body attack the fetus – it is unknown why. Some people speculate it is that the antibodies cross the placenta and cause a reaction. There is no test to figure out what percentage of women react this way – and is monitored very poorly because most people don't know this can happen – so we have no data on how often this actually happens.

Immunology textbooks still correctly point out that RhoGam should be given after childbirth only if the baby is Rh+. These are the mothers that are at high risk.
Doctors try to rationalize this by saying that even during the first pregnancy blood can mix and antibodies can be produced that will attack the baby. This almost never happens because the blood would have to mix twice, once to stimulate the production of Antibodies in the mother and a second time for those antibodies to diffuse to the baby.

Regardless, the paradox comes into play because if the mother's antibodies can diffuse to harm the baby, then so can the injected RhoGam antibodies. They are the same exact antibodies. Ask your doctor how your anti-Rh antibodies were more harmful than other mothers' anti-Rh antibodies (in Rhogam).

Each RhoGam injection also contains blood serum pooled from several different persons with the antibodies. The manufacturer cannot possibly screen or remove all viruses from it. But that's a separate issue.

The truth is – most women do not need the shot. Especially during the first pregnancy. With the first pregnancy the blood almost always mixes and causes the sensitization during the birthing process – meaning the baby is already out of the mom and there is no danger to it and no need for the shot during your first pregnancy.

You can also get a titer check to see if you have become sensitized and would even possibly want to consider it in your second pregnancy. If you haven't been sensitized, then there is very little reason to consider needing the shot.

As I state throughout the book – I am not saying to **not** get the Rhogam shot – I am just helping you be aware of the pros, cons, and who actually needs it. Our doctor (while an amazing guy) had no idea who actually needed Rhogam or not – it was just something they gave to everyone. He was professional enough to look into it and found out since both of us were Rh negative we certainly wouldn't need it – but think of how many people that didn't need it are given it daily across the country.

Pretty sweet for the pharmaceutical company that makes it though, huh? That doesn't even include the huge variables of unknowns that come from taking it.

People who don't exactly trust these companies – it **would** be a really sweet way to modify the genetics of every person in the country without them knowing.

I mean – both Merck and GSK – the largest suppliers of vaccines – have been weaponizing mycoplasmas since the 40s and testing them on large populations like prisons and orphans (YouTube Garth Nicolson and mycoplasmas for more). Or head over here to find out a little bit about vaccine contamination:

http://articles.mercola.com/sites/articles/archive/2010/04/17/major-vaccine-suspended-due-to-contamination-with-pig-virus.aspx

That, however, is a different topic for a different book – I'm just raising awareness is all.

Titanium Dioxide

Titanium Dioxide is a frequently nanoparticle sized particle added to coffee creamers, vitamins, supplements, sunscreens, foods, and other ingestible items. Its primary purpose is to make the substance appear "super white" – or to have an extra white and clean appearance.

The problem is, the FDA has currently dropped the ball completely on nanoparticle regulation of food and supplement additives and doesn't have any standards or regulations on them at all, despite them having been around for over 20 years.

Titanium dioxide is known to be carcinogenic, induce DNA strand breakage, oxidative stress, mitochondrial damage, increased reactive oxygen species generation, brain cell death, as well as disrupting gut health and altering gene expression.

The biggest problem comes with the supplements, coffee creamer, and food additives — because as these go down the digestive tract and end up in the same location very nearly that the fetus us.

With the problems discussed above, this become especially concerning in regards to a fetus being so close to the area where they would get absorbed and possibly migrate over to the baby. The thing is — no one knows because these studies have not been done. Nanoparticle pieces of metal were just added to things without giving any foresight to the consequences (which some could speculate was done on purpose).

The other problem that we have is — we have no idea how these things respond to EMF frequencies either, and if these further complicate the health dangers that are posed from them. Also, we don't know if someone drinks a coffee or takes their calcium pills that are filled with these nanoparticles and then goes to get an ultrasound what implications this has.

The least we can do is let you be aware of it — so you can choose coffee creamers that don't have this added, supplements that don't have this added (because it serves absolutely no biological function but to make your pills and creamer look really white), and avoid it where you can to minimize your risk.

It's almost like having a baby takes a conscious effort to protect the unborn baby huh?

Here's a few studies to help you see what we're talking about:

Assessment of evidence for nanosized titanium dioxide-generated DNA strand breaks and oxidatively damaged DNA in cells and animal models.
https://www.ncbi.nlm.nih.gov/pubmed/29172839

Gene expression profiling in colon of mice exposed to food additive titanium dioxide
https://www.ncbi.nlm.nih.gov/pubmed/29128614

Amplification of arsenic genotoxicity by TiO2 nanoparticles in mammalian cells: new insights from physicochemical interactions and mitochondria.

https://www.ncbi.nlm.nih.gov/pubmed/29046140

Reduction of oxidative damages induced by titanium dioxide nanoparticles correlates with induction of the Nrf2 pathway by GSPE supplementation in mice.

https://www.ncbi.nlm.nih.gov/pubmed/28780322

In vitro uptake and toxicity studies of metal nanoparticles and metal oxide nanoparticles in human HT29 cells.

https://www.ncbi.nlm.nih.gov/pubmed/28466231

Rosmarinus officinalis L. ameliorates titanium dioxide nanoparticles and induced some toxic effects in rats' blood.

https://www.ncbi.nlm.nih.gov/pubmed/28361401

Titanium dioxide nanoparticles: an in vitro study
of DNA binding, chromosome aberration assay, and comet
assay.

https://www.ncbi.nlm.nih.gov/pubmed/28050721

Genotoxicity and gene expression analyses of liver and lung
tissues of mice treated with titanium dioxide nanoparticles.

https://www.ncbi.nlm.nih.gov/pubmed/28011748

Chapter 3

Childbirth

Pitocin

This product – while commonly used – is not a pretty picture. You are far better off using Clary Sage Oil (which is a bioidentical oxytocin stimulator) or other natural means of stimulating labor and childbirth.

The problem is – not a lot of doctors actually understand hormones well – let alone synthetic vs. natural hormones. A synthetic version NEVER works the same as a natural one, and always, **always** has consequences.

The first consequence of this is decreased ability for the child to bond with its mother. Since a synthetic version of the hormone oxytocin is used, the mother will stop producing her own oxytocin – which is the trust and bonding hormone – especially between a newborn and its mother.

When the synthetic version is used, it signals the mother's body to stop producing her own. So while it may help induce labor – it shuts off the mother's hormone production because it fools the body into thinking it has enough – causing the mother's natural oxytocin levels to plummet. This is devastating to the breastfeeding time for both mother and child.

Recent studies have also found that it is linked to drastic increases in postpartum depression and anxiety as well. The figures reported are about a 30-40% increase in both – however the studies have just started coming out so the numbers are likely far higher due to doctors telling girls "it's all in your head" – because they are unaware of the link. It's not exactly the doctor's fault, because pharmaceutical companies either A.)

Don't look for this, or B.) Sweep the results under the rug. Sorry – fact of life of what really happens.

Also both recent – and long past – research shows that brain function and sexual preference is highly determined by oxytocin (or Pitocin). So while I'm not making any claims here (because these studies don't exist yet) – one could speculate that synthetic versions could certainly have an impact on sexual preference later in life. It could also change the way the baby's brain develops in response to bonding with the mother, other humans, trust levels – the list is very extensive.

The big problem is – none of these studies have ever been done. Mostly due to the ignorance of much of the medical community thinking that a synthetic hormone is the same as a natural one. Once again not exactly their fault – these sorts of things are suppressed on purpose on many different levels. Profits over people is nothing new.

There is another lady who I listened to give a talk. It was an exceptionally disturbing one so I won't mention exactly which one it was – but I will only talk about some of the information she provided. The research she spoke of came all the way back from the 1940s by the pedophile Alfred Kinsey.

Kinsey pioneered human sexuality research by proving that infants and children could orgasm – so they must be capable of consensual sexuality. He would measure how many times he could get infants to orgasm in a given amount of time – even if they were crying from being overexerted from it. This guy was messed up beyond belief – yet founded the sex education of modern America. Sorry to be the guy to tell you all of this – but this is reality, folks.

His research also found that if he used the hormone oxytocin along with opioids (epidurals) that it would provoke cross-species mating urges and promote homosexuality as well in animals.

As disturbing as all of this is – I point it out only because we do the exact same thing in modern medical procedures. Synthetic oxytocin, along with opioids (epidurals) on the regular.

So here's the thing. If we knew since the 40s that this would happen in animals – it certainly is worth questioning what exactly does it do to people? Oxytocin is very well documented to induce many forms of brain changes – and these studies are on the natural version – we have honestly no idea what happens with a synthetic version.

Problem is – I don't have those answers. Only the questions. And now you have those same questions you can ask and research as well. You don't have to believe me – you can look it all up yourself. Don't shoot the messenger.

Finally I encourage you to look up women's experiences with Pitocin on the internet. Many of them are not so good.

Many people also have raised the argument that Pitocin increases the risk of a need for a C-Section due to contractions being too strong or uncontrolled due to unnatural stimulation from an artificial hormone – and even crushing baby's heads and cutting off blood flow from said uncontrolled contractions.

Now that I've given you PTSD from this topic – let's move on.

Vitamin K Shot

First, in order to absorb vitamin K we have to have a functioning biliary and pancreas system. Your infant's digestive system isn't fully developed at birth which is why we give babies breastmilk (and delay solids) until they are at least 6 months old, and why breastmilk only contains a small amount of highly absorbable vitamin K.

Too much vitamin K could tax the liver and cause brain damage (among other things). As baby ages and the digestive tract, mucosal lining, gut flora, and enzyme functions develop, baby can process more vitamin K. Low levels of vitamin K at birth just...makes...sense???

Secondly, cord blood contains stem cells, which protect a baby against bleeding and perform all sorts of needed repairs inside an infant's body. Here's the kicker, in order for a baby to get this protective boost of stem cells, cord-cutting needs to be delayed and the blood needs to remain thin so stem cells can easily travel and perform their functions. Imagine that, baby has his/her own protective mechanism to prevent bleeding and repair organs...that wasn't discovered until after we started routinely giving infants vitamin K injections.

Third, a newborn might have low levels of vitamin K because its intestines are not yet colonized with bacteria needed to synthesize it and the "vitamin K cycle" isn't fully functional in newborns. It makes sense then to bypass the gut and inject vitamin K right into the muscle, right? Except baby's kidneys aren't fully functional either.

Fourth, babies are born with low levels of vitamin K compared to adults, but this level is still sufficient to prevent problems; vitamin K prophylaxis isn't necessarily needed.

Finally, several clinical observations support the hypothesis that children have natural protective mechanisms that justify their low vitamin K levels at birth.

I don't know about you, but we should probably figure out why that is before we "inject now and worry about it later."

Do you know why vitamin K is pushed on parents and their children? Because pharmaceutical companies don't like to lose money, doctors don't like to be questioned, the American Academy of Pediatrics dare not change its recommendations.

Baby's blood thickened with vitamin K causes a situation where stem cells have to move through sludge, not nicely greased blood vessels full of blood which can allow stem cells easy access to anywhere. Maybe one day it will dawn on the medical community that not only are cord blood stem cells important and useful to the newborn baby, but that stem cells need to thin blood for a reason.

Any fetus which gets being wrung out like a wet towel while traveling down a narrow drainpipe can incur damage in any part of the body, including in the brain, and needs an in-built fix-it. And stem cells cross the brain-blood barrier. In fact, stem cells can go ... anywhere!!! Amazing, don't you think? God's design has solutions for situational problems. Three solutions, actually. The second is the fact that naturally, in the first few days, a baby's blood clotting factors are lower than normal.

But modern medicine considers this a "defect" so we regularly want vitamin K which results in blood nearly 100 times thicker than an adult's. This vitamin K injection, so they say ... (like they say immediate cord clamping is safe, and normal, and delayed cord clamping is an unproven intervention) is because the baby wasn't designed right, and if you don't give a vitamin K injection, the baby "could bleed to death".

But there is an unanswered question:

"Why are blood clotting factors in babies low in the first few days after birth? Why has a baby got much thinner blood as a result?" Why has it been this way since the beginning of time?

Might a logical hypothesis be that thinner blood allows freer and quicker access of cord blood stem cells to any part of the body damaged during birth? After all, why should stem cells have to fight through a baby's blood which is now 100 times thicker than any adult's, courtesy of another needle?

Here's another problem:

The vitamin K shot is high in Polysorbate 80 (which is used in animal experiments to open the blood-brain barrier). This becomes an especially large issue when the hepatitis B shot comes along with its incredibly high levels of aluminum (more on this in later chapters). Hep B not yet gwee in UK

The thing is – giving a known neurotoxin (aluminum) along with a substance that opens up the blood-brain barrier......might not be a good idea.

To illustrate this point – the United States has the highest first day (and overall) infant mortality rate of any first world country, and even some second world countries. Virtually no other country in the world gives these two "interventions" like the United States does.

Also – vitamin K requires vitamin C to do its job. Without it – the liver can be damaged due to a nutrient imbalance (and we're not even talking the synthetics of it yet).

Another thing to ask your doctor – is would they recommend if every person went home and injected 20,000% of the daily recommended dose of any vitamin indiscriminately to a baby?

Would it be a good idea to give 20,000% of any vitamin to any person? That's the levels that are in the vitamin K shot. So if your doctor is against every other extreme dose of a vitamin (which they should be in most circumstances) – why do they make an exception here? Your doctor may have good reasoning – just be sure to ask.

I'm just throwing out the idea that just maybe – not every single baby born in the United States needs to have a vitamin K shot. There may be times – but does YOUR baby meet the criteria? Or is it something that "we just do"?

The vitamin K shot also contains benzyl alcohol which can disrupt the liver – and some of the side effects include respiratory and cardiac distress – along with **jaundice** – one of the things it's supposed to help avoid.

I'm not going to say I have the answers to all of these questions – but I do like to have people ask questions. Ask enough so you make the right decision for you.

I would also like to point out that you can get an oral solution of vitamin K that is far safer than the injected method if you need – there are many places online that make it – and will try to have the links put up eventually on our informational website. Oral vitamin K given to mothers who breastfeed is an effective way to get vitamin K to babies as well.

- The reasons people WOULD however need a vitamin K shot are:

  Maternal Use of Medications, Including Antibiotics – "Antibiotics, particularly a class known as cephalosporins, reduce the absorption of vitamin K in the body. Long-term use (more than 10 days) of antibiotics may result in vitamin K deficiency because these drugs kill not only harmful bacteria but also beneficial, vitamin K-activating bacteria. This is most likely to occur in people who already have low levels of vitamin K or are at risk for deficiency (such as those who are malnourished, elderly, or taking warfarin). Other medications can also interfere with vitamin K."

- **Certain Health Conditions** – If baby has undiagnosed cholestasis (liver problems), diarrhea, hepatitis, cystic fibrosis (CF), celiac disease, or alpha – 1-antitrypsin deficiency, or a genetic variation affecting vitamin K absorption, they may be at increased risk for VKDB.

Other factors are preterm delivery, low birth weight, and possibly traumatic delivery. Antibiotics given to a newborn may also affect their ability to generate vitamin K2 within their digestive tract.

For more than a century, many physicians have maintained a denial of infant pain, based on ancient prejudices and "scientific evidence" that was long ago disproven.

Many have made claims that newborns don't feel pain, or remember it, the way adults do. Not only do infants feel pain, but the earlier they experience it, the more damaging and longer lasting the psychological effects may be. Dr. David B. Chamberlain, psychologist and co-founder of the Association of Pre-and Perinatal Psychology and Health, wrote in his article "Babies Don't Feel Pain":

A Century of Denial in Medicine. *The earlier an infant is subjected to pain, the greater the potential for harm. Early pains include being born prematurely into a man-made 'womb,' being born full-term in a man-made delivery room, being subject to any surgery (major or minor), and being circumcised. We must alert the medical community to the psychological hazards of early pain and call for the removal of all man-made pain surrounding birth.*

Back in 1999, *Science Daily* published an article about the findings of a research team at the Washington School of Medicine that newborns who are exposed to a series of painful treatments display a variety of long-term effects as older children, including an altered response to pain and an exaggerated stress response. A 2004 study found that very early pain or stress experiences have long-lasting adverse consequences for newborns, including changes in the central nervous system and changes in responsiveness of the neuroendocrine and immune systems at maturity (remember this part when we come up to circumcision in a little bit).

Similarly, a 2008 study of analgesia in newborns and children concluded: *Healthy newborns routinely experience acute pain during blood sampling for metabolic screening, injection of vitamin K or hepatitis vaccine, or circumcision. Acute pain caused by skin-breaking procedures can lead to physiologic instability and behavioral distress, and it has downstream effects on subsequent pain processing, development and stress responsivity. Because of these detrimental effects, reduction and prevention of pain are worthy clinical goals that are also expected by most parents.*

In addition to the above, the possible trauma from the injection can jeopardize the establishment of breastfeeding, which is detrimental to both mother and baby.
https://www.ncbi.nlm.nih.gov/pmc/articles/PMC2464482/

Each insert for the vitamin K shot also states:

"Studies to evaluate the mutagenic potential have not been conducted with Vitamin K1 Injection.

Studies to evaluate the carcinogenic potential have not been conducted with Vitamin K1 Injection."

"In 1990 Golding et al[2] reported a study of a 1970 birth cohort in Britain in which they noted an unexpected association between childhood cancer and pethidine given in labor and the neonatal administration of vitamin K. Subsequently, Golding and others conducted a case-control study designed to examine the risk of cancer associated with intramuscular vitamin K administration among infants born in two hospitals in Avon between 1965 and 1987 and diagnosed with cancer between 1971 and 1989."
http://pediatrics.aappublications.org/content/91/5/1001
https://www.ncbi.nlm.nih.gov/pmc/articles/PMC1971807/

Delayed Cord Clamping

Fortunately this is starting to become the norm in hospitals as of late. This one is one of the least controversial of all topics – so I won't spend a lot of time on it.

A couple of extra minutes attached to the umbilical cord at birth may translate into a small boost in neurodevelopment several years later, a study suggests.

Children whose cords were cut more than three minutes after birth had slightly higher social skills and fine motor skills than those whose cords were cut within 10 seconds. The results showed no differences in IQ.

There is growing evidence from a number of studies that all infants, those born at term and those born early, benefit from receiving extra blood from the placenta at birth.

Delaying the clamping of the cord allows more blood to transfer from the placenta to the infant, sometimes increasing the infant's blood volume by up to a third. The iron in the blood increases infants' iron storage, and iron is essential for healthy brain development.

The extra blood at birth helps the baby to cope better with the transition from life in the womb, where everything is provided for them by the placenta and the mother, to the outside world and their lungs get more blood so that the exchange of oxygen into the blood can take place smoothly.

Basically – delaying cord clamping allows babies to get all the blood that's supposed to be theirs. Unless there's a clear reason to cut it early, I would highly suggest thinking about delaying it. The delay time can be anywhere from 3-5 minutes to get the full benefit – be sure to look into it more for yourself and see what is best for you.

Whilest pulsating the blood is returning to the baby taking stem cells with it.

Immediate Skin-to-Skin Contact

This one is a no-brainer. Unless you have an extreme need not to – get the baby on Mom's skin ASAP for loads of benefits. This also is becoming very standard care fortunately.

Strep B Antibiotics

Sometimes called GBS, Group B streptococcus is a common bacteria that is often found in the digestive tract and lower genital tract. It is considered a normal part of our microbiome and most people have no symptoms related to its presence. However, newborns affected by it are at risk for developing Group B strep disease, a potentially serious illness.

There are two forms of Group B strep disease in babies: early-onset and late-onset. About 80% of cases are early-onset, which means the illness occurs within seven days of birth, usually within the first 24 hours of life.

The remaining 20% happen between seven days and three months of age – this is referred to as late-onset. "Late-onset GBS infection is more complex and has not been convincingly tied to the GBS status of the mother." In other words, babies who develop late-onset GBS may have acquired it from their environment.

DOES EVERY BABY BORN TO A GBS+ MOTHER DEVELOP AN INFECTION?

No. Even without intervention many GBS+ women will give birth to babies that do not experience any complications. In one Canadian study, 19.5% of women tested at 36 weeks were positive for GBS. Left untreated, about 50% of those women passed GBS on to their babies, but 48-49% percent of the children who were colonized with GBS had no symptoms and 1-2% developed early-onset Group B strep disease. This however isn't the full picture – it is only one study – and we will of course try to add more details as they become available.

WHAT FACTORS INCREASE THE CHANCES OF ACTUAL INFECTION?

The three most significant factors for early-onset GBS are:

- fever during labor

- the woman's water breaks 18 hours or more before delivery (this is also known as prolonged rupture of membranes, or PROM)
- preterm birth (before 37 weeks) or broken water before 37 weeks gestation

So the thing is – just because you have Strep B doesn't mean it will become an issue – but you should personally weigh the risks.

Also – mothers with Strep B can pass immunity onto their children – meaning that unless you are immune deficient, you very possibly could pass the immunity to the Strep B onto your child.

Another study found that 61% of early-onset GBS cases occurred in babies whose moms tested negative for GBS. It's not clear why this is, but it may be because, as mentioned above, hospital stay transmissions of Strep B are well documented.

Finally – the most important piece of information:
According to a Cochrane Review (and others), the death rate from GBS remains the same whether or not antibiotics are administered. There was a reduction of babies who became ill, but mortality rates were not affected when IV antibiotics were administered.

Furthermore, the Cochrane Review concluded that very few women who are GBS+ give birth to babies who become infected with Group B strep disease, and "antibiotics can have harmful effects such as severe maternal allergic reactions, increase in drug-resistant organisms and exposure of newborn infants to resistant bacteria, and postnatal maternal and neonatal yeast infections. This review finds that giving antibiotics is not supported by conclusive evidence."

Antibiotics may also make babies more vulnerable to superbugs

Why is it that both the chlorhexidine wash and IV antibiotics seem to reduce the rate of GBS colonization (and in some studies illness) but not deaths? One theory is that while these methods do kill <u>most</u> GBS bacteria, a certain number may have mutated in a way that makes them resistant to antibiotics. When these strains are left behind, they band together to form a superbug – an infection that is resistant to one or more antibiotics. Essentially, the idea is that you take a relatively harmless colony – something like a small town with cooks, bakers, schoolteachers, etc. – and through antibiotic administration eliminate everyone but the soldiers.

Obviously, a band of soldiers is more likely to win a battle than a band of bakers. (As a note: Most antibiotic-resistant bacteria are not necessarily soldiers – a.k.a. more dangerous than other types when they start out. However, they can become dangerous simply because they are difficult to stop.)

Once again – I am not saying **NOT** to get IV antibiotics – I am saying to weigh all of your options.

Eye Ointment

Once again of all the options you could do – this is one of the least important ones in my opinion. Compared to everything else – this is just one of the most minimally invasive with the least amount of complications either way.

The eye ointment is usually given to avoid infections that are caused by gonorrhea and chlamydia. Since nearly every woman is screened for that during pregnancy – the risk of those causing what are the majority of eye infections in infants is extremely low. Chances are if you're reading this book – you probably know if you have either of those.

It can be used as well to avoid other infections such as E. coli infections in the eyes – but it is possible to wait and see if anything arises later and treat it then. Even the most "Green" parents should be able to notice if the infant's eyes get crusty and infected – so the risk of waiting, as long as you pay any sort of attention to your child, is low.

An argument to be made is that the eye drops have little actual effect/outcome on infection rates in most circumstances – and can contribute to antibiotic-resistant infections. It is after all an antibiotic – look at the shape America is in from giving antibiotics constantly – superbugs are rampant in the country.

That being said – there are very little side effects from using it. So out of all the decisions you have with a pregnancy – this one is not one that I'd put at the top of the "to worry too hard about" list.

Circumcision

Instead of using the term "circumcised" I'm going to be using the more accurate terms of "mutilated" and "intact" instead of "circumcised" and "uncircumcised".

It used to be thought, and was the original medical reason for male genital mutilation - was that it reduced the risk of infection, STD's, cured AIDS, cured schizophrenia, prevented masturbation, along with a whole host of what could now be considered outrageous claims. On top of that – mutilated men are 4.5x more likely to have erectile dysfunction later in life as well.
https://www.psychologytoday.com/blog/moral-

landscapes/201109/circumcision-social-sexual-psychological-realities

It also used to be thought that mutilated boys would have lower rates of genital infections during childhood – but the only way this turned out to be even remotely true was because doctors were improperly trained to pull back the foreskin prematurely to clean it. The foreskin is instead meant not to retract until it is fully ready – and retracting it prematurely lead to the majority of infections that occurred in boys (in which the studies used to use to justify the mutilation)

Outside of the fact that intact infants have no higher rate of infections, male genital mutilation also does not prevent the spread of STDs in any way, shape, or form. (https://academic.oup.com/jid/article/200/3/370/900692/Adult-Male-Circumcision-Does-Not-Reduce-the-Risk)

Here's another comparison I'd like you to make. Let's say that it **DID** prevent any infections in newborns – it would make more sense to remove every girl's breasts at birth to prevent breast cancer – than it would to mutilate every boy's genitals.

Now bear with me here – that may sound outrageous.

It is – but in reality it's true. 1 in 3 women now get breast cancer – nowhere near 1 in 3,000 intact boys gets a genital infection – so by the numbers it would make 1000x more sense to remove every girl's breasts at birth.

Mutilated men experience 60% less sexual pleasure on average than intact men. Being a guy – I could certainly go for 60% more pleasure. My wife might get even more annoyed with my advances due to them being more frequent – but I suppose that's a price at least I am willing to pay.

Circumcision is also exceptionally traumatic to the child.

What that level of pain and trauma does – is fragments the mind into two (or more) pieces. Part of the mind has to essentially retreat from the body to avoid having to deal with the trauma – in essence creating "two" personalities. It's more like creating a personality and a sub-personality, but those are just semantics. It is a tactic used in what is called MK Ultra and Operation Monarch to create large enough amounts of childhood trauma to fracture a personality.

This trauma then wires a man for a life of self destruction and self depreciation – partly because the first time this little boy connected with his penis – is when the tip of it was being cut off. Anesthetics can be used, yes – but they often don't work very well – if at all.

Many psychologists also argue that this is one of the reasons that you very rarely will see an intact male in a porno – because of the innate higher level of self respect that an intact male has over a mutilated one.

Brain scans of babies undergoing genital mutilation show them lighting up like a Christmas tree with pain signals – even if anesthesia was used (many doctors joke that the anesthesia is for the parents to make them feel better). This also creates a circumstance where the man will have "less respect" for that part of his body, due to it being damaged already.

The sexuality isn't the only thing that's effected either. This also hardwires the brain for a greater propensity for fear and anger.

Something to note – is that it shouldn't be held against any parents that simply just didn't know any of this.

The narrative is so well controlled by certain parties that I expect a huge amount of backlash from this topic. I welcome it – because I understand. It took me quite a while to come to terms with this whole topic.

Another thing that happens is these trauma pathways are re-activated and strengthened in boys who are sexually abused. It causes the trauma centers to re-light up – making mutilated boys far more susceptible to the long-term effects of molestation.

Many people will argue "well I don't want him made fun of in the locker room". If we all came to terms with the fact that mutilating every young boy's penis isn't such a great idea – the harassment would naturally go away nearly instantly. A comparable argument to boys being teased for being intact would be "we should give every flat chested girl breast implants so they don't get made fun of". You can decide when you compare it that way if it still makes any sense.

There's also the "we want the boy to look like daddy" argument – which is essentially "we should traumatize the child in order to spare the father's feelings". It would make far more sense to explain to the child why you decided not to mutilate their genitals – even if the fathers were.

Also – the remains of the mutilated foreskin are often sold and turned into an expensive face cream. That thought alone disturbs me personally enough that I wouldn't have even needed to read the rest of this topic to make my decision.

I understand this is probably a very tough section to read – I do.

If you've already done it to one of your children – please don't use that as an excuse to keep doing it. It's like saying you cut off one arm – so you might as well cut the other one off too.

I'm not saying this because I hold any judgment – mostly because people aren't told these things.

This is one of the few places in the book where I will put the links right here as well as the back of the book – for you to explore the topic further – because I feel it is extremely important. You can also hit up Google and scholar.google.com to find thousands of other studies just like these.

https://www.psychologytoday.com/blog/moral-landscapes/201109/myths-about-circumcision-you-likely-believe

https://www.psychologytoday.com/blog/moral-landscapes/201501/circumcision-s-psychological-damage

http://www.cirp.org/library/psych/

"We justify male infant circumcision by pretending that the babies don't feel it because they're too young and it will have no consequences when they are older. This is not true. Women who experience memories of abuse in childhood know how deeply and painfully early experiences leave their marks in the body. Why wouldn't the same thing apply to boys?"

Christiane Northrup, M.D

"Changes in infant-maternal interaction have been observed after circumcision, including disrupted feeding and weaker attachment between the infant and mother. The American Academy of Pediatrics Task Force on Circumcision noted behavioral changes resulting from circumcision in their report. The behavior of nearly 90 percent of circumcised infants has been found to be significantly changed after the circumcision. Differences in sleep patterns and more irritability – both signs of stress – have been observed among circumcised infants."

http://www.doctorsopposingcircumcision.org/for-professionals/psychological-impact/

Finally – recent studies are showing that circumcision doubles the risk of autism in boys. This may partially explain why boys have so much higher risk of autism than girls. It is also worth noting that this study involved over 300,000 boys – so the it was

an extremely large study:
http://www.telegraph.co.uk/men/active/mens-health/11334800/Circumcision-doubles-autism-risk-study-claims.html

Finally – if your child grows up and really wants to be circumcised – they have the option to do so then.

You can't undo it once it's done.

Cry it out

The "Cry it out" method got its roots back in the 1880's when germs were first discovered and the notion was that "babies should rarely be touched".

Men of science in their infinite wisdom decided that they knew better than mothers and grandmothers on how to raise a child. The decided that too much attention would a make a child "whiney, dependent, and a failed human being." They even released a pamphlet around the same time saying "mothering meant holding the baby quietly, in tranquility-inducing positions" and that "the mother should stop immediately if her arms feel tired" because "the baby is never to inconvenience the adult."

A baby older than six months "should be taught to sit silently in the crib; otherwise, he might need to be constantly watched and entertained by the mother, a serious waste of time." Is what was taught at this time.

Using modern neuroscience imaging, we can confirm common sense that **letting babies get distressed is a practice that can damage children and their relational capacities in many ways for the long term**.

We know now – as common sense and maternal instinct has always known - that leaving babies to cry is a good way to make a less intelligent, less healthy but more anxious, uncooperative and alienated persons who can pass the same or worse traits on to the next generation.

Rats are often used to study how mammalian brains work and many effects are similar in human brains. In studies of rats with high or low nurturing mothers, there is a critical period for turning on genes that control anxiety for the rest of life. If in the first 10 days of life you have a low nurturing rat mother (the equivalent of the first 6 months of life in a human), the gene never gets turned on and the rat is anxious towards new situations for the rest of its life, unless drugs are administered to alleviate the anxiety.

This concept is basically a pharmaceutical's wet dream right here – which is probably why it is commonly taught in medical school that the "cry it out method" is "safe and effective".

Any time you hear that term you should have a lot of red flags going off – but that's just my thoughts.

The long story short of all the science is – that caregivers drastically shape the way genes are turned on and off depending upon how a child is raised, in both animals and in humans. Nature vs Nurture – well nurture plays a large hand in epigenetic expression.

Let's play a simple thought experiment together.

You're a brand new baby thrust into a new world. You've been for your entire life up until this point – been in a womb where your every need has been met instantly. You have the sound of your mother's heartbeat 24 hours a day, and the sound of her voice for all of her waking hours.

You feel what she feels, eat what she eats, and go where she goes. There is no separation. It's always warm, comfortable, and you're in a state of near virtual suspension.

Upon birth you're thrust into a cold world, where your mother's voice isn't always around. The sound of her heartbeat is heard only when nursing, and you're not held 24 hours a day, but only for select periods of time.

When you need something – you do the only thing you can. You cry. And when you cry whatever need it is you have is usually met fairly rapidly and comfort and food is delivered.

Breastfed babies have the sound of mom's heartbeat to soothe them while they eat, and help them go to sleep.

Now fast forward to doctor recommended idea of "cry it out". When it comes time that you're alone in a dark, scary, cold world devoid of the mother's heartbeat – you need something (doesn't matter what it is or how irrelevant it might seem that you're simply "missing mom") and you start to cry.

Up until now your cries have been answered, but this time your cries go unanswered. So you have to options – to cry harder or stop crying. Since you still need something, and that's why you're crying – you cry harder. This escalates the stress hormones and can rapidly bring them up high. Now you're crying, you're stressed out, and no one is there. You cry harder. As your cries go unnoticed in the dark, they fall upon deaf ears because the doctor said to just let you cry. You cry harder – wondering what you have done that your parents won't come to your side to help comfort you or satisfy your needs.

Enough time goes by – you finally fall asleep from exhaustion, and the damage has been done. You now have something called "learned helplessness", where you have learned to stop asking for help.

It's much like the elephant at the circus – after a while of tying the elephant up to a pole from which it cannot break away from (called "breaking" the elephant), it simply stops trying. You could tie the elephant to a plastic chair and it wouldn't attempt to move it (even though it easily could) because it has learned to be helpless and quit trying.

This is what happens inside of your baby's mind when the "cry it out method" – the baby learns to stop asking for help when something is wrong, and this carries over into adulthood with dire consequences.

Let's be honest here – doctors are not psychologists/psychiatrists, and many of them think the answer to a problem is medication and not addressing the reason for the cause.

What we literally have here is a clever, damaging method to set a child up for the need for medication for the rest of their life. This bodes quite well for pharmaceutical companies now doesn't it? I suppose this might be a reason for having it be the "doctor approved" method that is taught in medical school – despite that it violates any and all common sense.

Rather than give you 100 links to follow, below is a single one that has every link and reason that you'll need to help you make the decision on if your doctor has lost their mind or not by recommending cry it out. You don't need a fancy medical degree to use some common sense and realize there might be a problem with this method.

That being said – at some point however parents will be unable to satisfy the screams of a colicky child, just be sure to make the correlation if the non-stop crying comes after round of vaccinations.

https://www.psychologytoday.com/blog/moral-landscapes/201112/dangers-crying-it-out

Birth to 2 years

While I did lump a few of the other topics that could have gone into this section – I put them previously in the book because this section will mostly focus on vaccination and "well baby visits".

I also want to make this perfectly clear – this is not an "anti-vaccine" section.

This is a section to paint the other side of the picture and use actual historical and scientific data.

While the majority of the research will be on the "other side" of the pharmaceutical narrative that vaccines are nothing but "safe and effective" – this is only because nearly everyone knows that side of the story.

There's billions and billions of dollars poured into astroturfing every year – so there's no shortage of being able to find that view.

What I **have** found is that these companies don't just astroturf. They write fake articles, skew data, re-interpret it until they get data they want, throw trashcan parties with data they don't like, rig Google's algorithms so only the studies that paint vaccines in favorable light show up before page 100 in a search, or the studies that don't fit their narrative slowly just start to disappear over time.

I am aware of all of this – because I've been doing the research on it for years. I'm not saying I know everything – but I can say – I notice www.pubmed.gov has fewer search results on the topics than it did a few months ago – or a few years ago.

I notice how much harder it is to find the same studies I look up over and over going to Google – and how they fall further and further (if they show up at all) down the query list.

There's also people who are paid huge sums of money like Paul Offit (who believes that an infant could handle 10,000 vaccines at once) – who just so happen to sell his rotavirus vaccine for million and millions of dollars (and sat on the CDC commission to get it introduced into the schedule) – and Senator Richard Pan who believes the most dangerous ingredient in vaccines is "water" and spearheaded a campaign to make vaccines mandatory to attend school in California.

I also would love to say that we could trust government agencies to do the right thing and be free of any outside influences – but I live in reality. Flint, Michigan can tell you all about that.

The biggest problem I have is that the CDC – who is responsible for making sure vaccines are safe – is listed in Dun and Bradstreet as a private – for profit – corporation – that receives money from the government. And while they are responsible for making sure vaccines are safe – they are simultaneously responsible for vaccine promotion as well – and own multiple patents on vaccines. A fox guarding the hen-house type of deal. I'm not saying to not trust them – I'm just saying *I* don't. Here is the link to their listing on Dun and Bradstreet:

https://businesscredit.dnb.com/coo/?companyName=CDC&state=GA&country=US&type=coo&utm_source=dnb-topsearch&api_key=5ZQdbHqkcAFmbERsDp2klim0edSV7oMb

I only say these things to point out to you that billions upon billions are spent every year to control the research and not only what gets said about vaccines – but what gets taught about them.

I aim only to share the studies from the opposite side of the table – and let you draw your own conclusions.

I'm not going to say vaccines cause autism – but I will tell you there are hundreds of papers out there that say they can/do.

Like everyone – I saw the little kid flipping around his empty folder of no research to link vaccines to autism on YouTube – it magically got quite popular (wonder how that happened). I can tell you – that kid needs to do some actual research. There are quite a few papers out there – and this book will include them.

Keep in mind that even with 100s of research papers saying that vaccines can cause autism – that doesn't mean they do. It could support the argument that vaccines can contribute to autism – but that doesn't mean they are the sole cause in any circumstance.

The important part is to work **WITH** your doctor – and ask any questions you have after reading this section of the book. The first section will actually be a list of questions to ask your doctor.

I'm going to attempt to write this so that you can ask basic, common-sense questions – to get answers that will help you make up your mind. You are of course welcome to read over all of the studies linked in this book as well – however I'm going to attempt to simplify it so you don't have to.

Of course – I always recommend you do read them all. I personally like this thing called "informed consent".

The more you can learn about your decision, the better chances you can make the right one for you – because you are the one who has to live with the consequences of that decision.

Starting questions to ask your doctor:

- How many hours of vaccine education have you received – specifically on each vaccine?

- Do you believe that vaccines are completely safe and effective?

- Do you have any studies showing the current CDC /NHS recommended vaccine schedule is safe?

- Do you believe that giving more than one vaccine at once is safe?

- If so – up to how many vaccines at once do you believe are safe to give in a single visit?

- Do you have any studies that can back up your opinion that more than one vaccine at once is safe?

- Do you do any screening to identify children who are at higher risk of being vaccine injured? HTMFR gene variation

- Do you give vaccines to kids currently sick?

- Do you give vaccines to kids who are currently on antibiotics?

- Do you screen children for allergies to substances in vaccines before giving them (such as egg, latex, yeast, neomycin, and so forth)?

- What studies did you use to justify vaccines exceeding the FDA's daily limits on aluminum?

  See Dr Chris Exley's research

- Would you be comfortable taking the current CDC's vaccine schedule yourself?

- Would you be comfortable adjusting that schedule for differences in weight and taking it (meaning taking 15 DTaP vaccines at once to account for larger body weight than an infant)?

- Do you screen for mitochondrial disorders prior to vaccination?

- Do you screen for genetic mutations like MTHFR that make kids unable to detoxify from vaccines and increases their likelihood of having an adverse reaction?

- Do you read your patients the insert before every vaccine and identify reactions they should watch for?

- Do you follow up after vaccinations to identify any adverse events and report them to VAERS?

- Do you have any studies that injecting every child with both male and female DNA from aborted fetuses is safe and doesn't affect sexuality or personal identity?

- Can you provide a purity test to ensure that vaccines are free from mycoplasmas, retroviruses, and parasites?

- Can you provide a purity to test to ensure the vaccine doesn't contain the weed-killer RoundUp?

- Can you provide a purity test to ensure the vaccine is not contaminated with other heavy metals during the manufacturing process?

- Do you have a test that can see the levels of aborted fetal tissue in vaccines containing aborted fetal tissue?

- What compensation do you receive from making sure my child is vaccinated?

Before we even start talking about vaccines, we just wanted to put something called the "excipient list" here right away so you could read the actual ingredients in vaccines for yourself. This is a topic that most doctors unfortunately are completely oblivious to – and as parents we were glad we were informed that vaccines contained animal DNA, insect DNA, and aborted fetal DNA – as well as so many other things. You are of course welcome to form your own opinion on what you think of these ingredients and be sure to research any you are unsure of. Yes, we know the pictures are small (best we can do – so we really highly suggest you download and look yourself), but you may even download this list for yourself at:

https://www.cdc.gov/vaccines/pubs/pinkbook/downloads/appendices/b/excipient-table-2.pdf

Vaccine Excipient & Media Summary
Excipients Included in U.S. Vaccines, by Vaccine

In addition to weakened or killed disease antigens (viruses or bacteria), vaccines contain very small amounts of other ingredients – excipients or media.

Some excipients are added to a vaccine for a specific purpose. These include:
Preservatives, to prevent contamination. For example, thimerosal.
Adjuvants, to help stimulate a stronger immune response. For example, aluminum salts.
Stabilizers, to keep the vaccine potent during transportation and storage. For example, sugars or gelatin.

Others are residual trace amounts of materials that were used during the manufacturing process and removed. These include:
Cell culture materials, used to grow the vaccine antigens. For example, egg protein, various culture media.
Inactivating ingredients, used to kill viruses or inactivate toxins. For example, formaldehyde.
Antibiotics, used to prevent contamination by bacteria. For example, neomycin.

The following table lists all components, other than antigens, shown in the manufacturers' package insert (PI) for each vaccine. Each of these PIs, which can be found on the FDA's website (see below) contains a description of that vaccine's manufacturing process, including the amount and purpose of each substance. In most PIs, this information is found in Section 11: "Description."

All information was extracted from manufacturers' package inserts, current as of January 6, 2017.
If in doubt about whether a PI has been updated since then, check the FDA's website at:
http://www.fda.gov/BiologicsBloodVaccines/Vaccines/ApprovedProducts/ucm093833.htm

Vaccine	Contains
Adenovirus	human-diploid fibroblast cell cultures (strain WI-38), Dulbecco's Modified Eagle's Medium, fetal bovine serum, sodium bicarbonate, monosodium glutamate, sucrose, D-mannose, D-fructose, dextrose, human serum albumin, potassium phosphate, plasdone C, anhydrous lactose, microcrystalline cellulose, polacrilin potassium, magnesium stearate, microcrystalline cellulose, magnesium stearate, cellulose acetate phthalate, alcohol, acetone, castor oil, FD&C Yellow #6 aluminum lake dye
Anthrax (Biothrax)	amino acids, vitamins, inorganic salts, sugars, aluminum hydroxide, sodium chloride, benzethonium chloride, formaldehyde
BCG (Tice)	glycerin, asparagine, citric acid, potassium phosphate, magnesium sulfate, iron ammonium citrate, lactose
Cholera (Vaxchora)	casamino acids, yeast extract, mineral salts, anti-foaming agent, ascorbic acid, hydrolyzed casein, sodium chloride, sucrose, dried lactose, sodium bicarbonate, sodium carbonate
DT (Sanofi)	aluminum phosphate, isotonic sodium chloride, formaldehyde, casein, cystine, maltose, uracil, inorganic salts, vitamins, dextrose
DTaP (Daptacel)	aluminum phosphate, formaldehyde, glutaraldehyde, 2-phenoxyethanol, Stainer-Scholte medium, casamino acids, dimethyl-beta-cyclodextrin, Mueller's growth medium, ammonium sulfate, modified Mueller-Miller casamino acid medium without beef heart infusion, 2-phenoxyethanol
DTaP (Infanrix)	Fenton medium containing a bovine extract, modified Latham medium derived from bovine casein, formaldehyde, modified Stainer-Scholte liquid medium, glutaraldehyde, aluminum hydroxide, sodium chloride, polysorbate 80 (Tween 80)
DTaP-IPV (Kinrix)	Fenton medium containing a bovine extract, modified Latham medium derived from bovine casein, formaldehyde, modified Stainer-Scholte liquid medium, glutaraldehyde, aluminum hydroxide, VERO cells, a continuous line of monkey kidney cells, Calf serum, lactalbumin hydrolysate, sodium chloride, polysorbate 80 (Tween 80), neomycin sulfate, polymyxin B
DTaP-IPV (Quadracel)	modified Mueller's growth medium, ammonium sulfate, modified Mueller-Miller casamino acid medium without beef heart infusion, formaldehyde, ammonium sulfate aluminum phosphate, Stainer-Scholte medium, casamino acids, dimethyl-beta-cyclodextrin, MRC-5 cells, normal human diploid cells, CMRL 1969 medium supplemented with calf serum, Medium 199 without calf serum, 2-phenoxyethanol, polysorbate 80, glutaraldehyde, neomycin, polymyxin B sulfate

Vaccine	Contains
DTaP-HepB-IPV (Pediarix)	Fenton medium containing a bovine extract, modified Latham medium derived from bovine casein, formaldehyde, modified Stainer-Scholte liquid medium, VERO cells, a continuous line of monkey kidney cells, calf serum and lactalbumin hydrolysate, aluminum hydroxide, aluminum phosphate, aluminum salts, sodium chloride, polysorbate 80 (Tween 80), neomycin sulfate, polymyxin B, yeast protein.
DTaP-IPV/Hib (Pentacel)	aluminum phosphate, polysorbate 80, sucrose, formaldehyde, glutaraldehyde, bovine serum albumin, 2-phenoxyethanol, neomycin, polymyxin B sulfate, modified Mueller's growth medium, ammonium sulfate, modified Mueller-Miller casamino acid medium without beef heart infusion, Stainer-Scholte medium, casamino acids, dimethyl-beta-cyclodextrin, glutaraldehyde, MRC-5 cells (a line of normal human diploid cells), CMRL 1969 medium supplemented with calf serum, Medium 199 without calf serum, modified Mueller and Miller medium
Hib (ActHIB)	sodium chloride, modified Mueller and Miller medium (the culture medium contains milk-derived raw materials [casein derivatives]), formaldehyde, sucrose
Hib (Hiberix)	saline, synthetic medium, formaldehyde, sodium chloride, lactose
Hib (PedvaxHIB)	complex fermentation media, amorphous aluminum hydroxyphosphate sulfate, sodium chloride
Hib/Mening. CY (MenHibrix)	saline, semi-synthetic media, formaldehyde, sucrose, tris (tromethamol)-HCl
Hep A (Havrix)	MRC-5 human diploid cells, formalin, aluminum hydroxide, amino acid supplement, phosphate-buffered saline solution, polysorbate 20, neomycin sulfate, aminoglycoside antibiotic
Hep A (Vaqta)	MRC-5 diploid fibroblasts, amorphous aluminum hydroxyphosphate sulfate, non-viral protein, DNA, bovine albumin, formaldehyde, neomycin, sodium borate, sodium chloride
Hep B (Engerix-B)	aluminum hydroxide, yeast protein, sodium chloride, disodium phosphate dihydrate, sodium dihydrogen phosphate dihydrate
Hep B (Recombivax)	soy peptone, dextrose, amino acids, mineral salts, phosphate buffer, formaldehyde, potassium aluminum sulfate, amorphous aluminum hydroxyphosphate sulfate, yeast protein
Hep A/Hep B (Twinrix)	MRC-5 human diploid cells, formalin, aluminum phosphate, aluminum hydroxide, amino acids, sodium chloride, phosphate buffer, polysorbate 20, neomycin sulfate, yeast protein
Human Papillomavirus (HPV) (Gardasil)	vitamins, amino acids, mineral salts, carbohydrates, amorphous aluminum hydroxyphosphate sulfate, sodium chloride, L-histidine, polysorbate 80, sodium borate, yeast protein
Human Papillomavirus (HPV) (Gardasil 9)	vitamins, amino acids, mineral salts, carbohydrates, amorphous aluminum hydroxyphosphate sulfate, sodium chloride, L-histidine, polysorbate 80, sodium borate, yeast protein
Influenza (Afluria) Trivalent & Quadrivalent	sodium chloride, monobasic sodium phosphate, dibasic sodium phosphate, monobasic potassium phosphate, potassium chloride, calcium chloride, sodium taurodeoxycholate, ovalbumin, sucrose, neomycin sulfate, polymyxin B, beta-propiolactone, thimerosal (multi-dose vials)
Influenza (Fluad)	squalene, polysorbate 80, sorbitan trioleate, sodium citrate dehydrate, citric acid monohydrate, neomycin, kanamycin, barium, egg proteins, CTAB (cetyltrimethylammonium bromide), formaldehyde
Influenza (Fluarix) Trivalent & Quadrivalent	octoxynol-10 (TRITON X-100), α-tocopheryl hydrogen succinate, polysorbate 80 (Tween 80), hydrocortisone, gentamicin sulfate, ovalbumin, formaldehyde, sodium deoxycholate, sodium phosphate-buffered isotonic sodium chloride
Influenza (Flublok) Trivalent & Quadrivalent	sodium chloride, monobasic sodium phosphate, dibasic sodium phosphate, polysorbate 20 (Tween 20), baculovirus and Spodoptera frugiperda cell proteins, baculovirus and cellular DNA, Triton X-100, lipids, vitamins, amino acids, mineral salts
Influenza (Flucelvax) Trivalent & Quadrivalent	Madin Darby Canine Kidney (MDCK) cell protein, protein other than HA, MDCK cell DNA, polysorbate 80, cetyltrimethlyammonium bromide, and β-propiolactone
Influenza (Flulaval) Trivalent & Quadrivalent	ovalbumin, formaldehyde, sodium deoxycholate, α-tocopheryl hydrogen succinate, polysorbate 80, thimerosal (multi-dose vials)
Influenza (Fluvirin)	ovalbumin, polymyxin, neomycin, betapropiolactone, nonylphenol ethoxylate, thimerosal
Influenza (Fluzone) Quadrivalent	formaldehyde, egg protein, octylphenol ethoxylate (Triton X-100), sodium phosphate-buffered isotonic sodium chloride solution, thimerosal (multi-dose vials), sucrose

Vaccine	Contains
Influenza (Fluzone) High Dose	egg protein, octylphenol ethoxylate (Triton X-100), sodium phosphate-buffered isotonic sodium chloride solution, formaldehyde, sucrose
Influenza (Fluzone) Intradermal	egg protein, octylphenol ethoxylate (Triton X-100), sodium phosphate-buffered isotonic sodium chloride solution, sucrose
Influenza (FluMist) Quadrivalent	monosodium glutamate, hydrolyzed porcine gelatin, arginine, sucrose, dibasic potassium phosphate, monobasic potassium phosphate, ovalbumin, gentamicin sulfate, ethylenediaminetetraacetic acid (EDTA)
Japanese Encephalitis (Ixiaro)	aluminum hydroxide, protamine sulfate, formaldehyde, bovine serum albumin, host cell DNA, sodium metabisulphite, host cell protein
Meningococcal (MenACWY-Menactra)	Watson Scherp media containing casamino acid, modified culture medium containing hydrolyzed casein, ammonium sulfate, sodium phosphate, formaldehyde, sodium chloride
Meningococcal (MenACWY-Menveo)	formaldehyde, amino acids, yeast extract, Franz complete medium, CY medium
Meningococcal (MPSV4-Menomune)	Mueller Hinton casein agar, Watson Scherp casamino acid media, thimerosal (multi-dose vials), lactose
Meningococcal (MenB – Bexsero)	aluminum hydroxide, E. coli, histidine, sucrose, deoxycholate, kanamycin
Meningococcal (MenB – Trumenba)	defined fermentation growth media, polysorbate 80, histidine buffered saline.
MMR (MMR-II)	chick embryo cell culture, WI-38 human diploid lung fibroblasts, vitamins, amino acids, fetal bovine serum, sucrose, glutamate, recombinant human albumin, neomycin, sorbitol, hydrolyzed gelatin, sodium phosphate, sodium chloride
MMRV (ProQuad) (Frozen)	chick embryo cell culture, WI-38 human diploid lung fibroblasts MRC-5 cells, sucrose, hydrolyzed gelatin, sodium chloride, sorbitol, monosodium L-glutamate, sodium phosphate dibasic, human albumin, sodium bicarbonate, potassium phosphate monobasic, potassium chloride; potassium phosphate dibasic, neomycin, bovine calf serum
MMRV (ProQuad) (Refrigerator Stable)	chick embryo cell culture, WI-38 human diploid lung fibroblasts, MRC-5 cells, sucrose, hydrolyzed gelatin, urea, sodium chloride, sorbitol, monosodium L-glutamate, sodium phosphate, recombinant human albumin, sodium bicarbonate, potassium phosphate potassium chloride, neomycin, bovine serum albumin
Pneumococcal (PCV13 – Prevnar 13)	soy peptone broth, casamino acids and yeast extract-based medium, CRM197 carrier protein, polysorbate 80, succinate buffer, aluminum phosphate
Pneumococcal (PPSV-23 – Pneumovax)	phenol
Polio (IPV – Ipol)	Eagle MEM modified medium, calf bovine serum, M-199 without calf bovine serum, vero cells (a continuous line of monkey kidney cells), phenoxyethanol, formaldehyde, neomycin, streptomycin, polymyxin B
Rabies (Imovax)	human albumin, neomycin sulfate, phenol red indicator, MRC-5 human diploid cells, beta-propriolactone
Rabies (RabAvert)	chicken fibroblasts, β-propiolactone, polygeline (processed bovine gelatin), human serum albumin, bovine serum, potassium glutamate, sodium EDTA, ovalbumin neomycin, chlortetracycline, amphotericin B
Rotavirus (RotaTeq)	sucrose, sodium citrate, sodium phosphate monobasic monohydrate, sodium hydroxide, polysorbate 80, cell culture media, fetal bovine serum, vero cells [DNA from porcine circoviruses (PCV) 1 and 2 has been detected in RotaTeq. PCV-1 and PCV-2 are not known to cause disease in humans.]
Rotavirus (Rotarix)	amino acids, dextran, Dulbecco's Modified Eagle Medium (sodium chloride, potassium chloride, magnesium sulfate, ferric (III) nitrate, sodium phosphate, sodium pyruvate, D-glucose, concentrated vitamin solution, L-cystine, L-tyrosine, amino acids solution, L-250 glutamine, calcium chloride, sodium hydrogenocarbonate, and phenol red), sorbitol, sucrose, calcium carbonate, sterile water, xanthan [Porcine circovirus type 1 (PCV-1) is present in Rotarix. PCV-1 is not known to cause disease in humans.]
Smallpox (Vaccinia – ACAM2000)	African Green Monkey kidney (Vero) cells, HEPES, human serum albumin, sodium chloride, neomycin, polymyxin B, Glycerin, phenol

Vaccine	Contains
Td (Tenivac)	aluminum phosphate, formaldehyde, modified Mueller-Miller casamino acid medium without beef heart infusion, ammonium sulfate
Td (Mass Biologics)	aluminum phosphate, formaldehyde, thimerosal, modified Mueller's media which contains bovine extracts, ammonium sulfate
Tdap (Adacel)	aluminum phosphate, formaldehyde, 2-phenoxyethanol, Stainer-Scholte medium, casamino acids, dimethyl-beta-cyclodextrin, glutaraldehyde, modified Mueller-Miller casamino acid medium without beef heart infusion, ammonium sulfate, modified Mueller's growth medium
Tdap (Boostrix)	modified Latham medium derived from bovine casein, Fenton medium containing a bovine extract, formaldehyde, modified Stainer-Scholte liquid medium, glutaraldehyde, aluminum hydroxide, sodium chloride, polysorbate 80
Typhoid (inactivated – Typhim Vi)	hexadecyltrimethylammonium bromide, formaldehyde, phenol, polydimethylsiloxane, disodium phosphate, monosodium phosphate, semi-synthetic medium
Typhoid (Vivotif Ty21a)	yeast extract, casein, dextrose, galactose, sucrose, ascorbic acid, amino acids, lactose, magnesium stearate, gelatin
Varicella (Varivax) *Frozen*	human embryonic lung cell cultures, guinea pig cell cultures, human diploid cell cultures (WI-38), human diploid cell cultures (MRC-5), sucrose, hydrolyzed gelatin, sodium chloride, monosodium L-glutamate, sodium phosphate dibasic, potassium phosphate monobasic, potassium chloride, EDTA (Ethylenediaminetetraacetic acid), neomycin, fetal bovine serum
Varicella (Varivax) *Refrigerator Stable*	human embryonic lung cell cultures, guinea pig cell cultures, human diploid cell cultures (WI-38), human diploid cell cultures (MRC-5), sucrose, hydrolyzed gelatin, urea, sodium chloride, monosodium L-glutamate, sodium phosphate dibasic, potassium phosphate monobasic, potassium chloride, neomycin, bovine calf serum
Yellow Fever (YF-Vax)	sorbitol, gelatin, sodium chloride, egg protein
Zoster (Shingles – Zostavax) *Frozen*	sucrose, hydrolyzed porcine gelatin, sodium chloride, monosodium L-glutamate, sodium phosphate dibasic, potassium phosphate monobasic, potassium chloride; MRC-5 cells, neomycin, bovine calf serum
Zoster (Shingles – Zostavax) *Refrigerator Stable*	sucrose, hydrolyzed porcine gelatin, urea, sodium chloride, monosodium L-glutamate, sodium phosphate dibasic, potassium phosphate monobasic, potassium chloride, MRC-5 cells, neomycin, bovine calf serum

A table listing vaccine excipients and media *by excipient* can be found in:

Grabenstein JD. *ImmunoFacts: Vaccines and Immunologic Drugs* – 2013
(38th revision). St Louis, MO: Wolters Kluwer Health, 2012.

Aluminum

Aluminum is commonly found in the earth's crust at a weight of about 8% elementally on the planet. Free form aluminum is almost never found anywhere on the planet except in rare circumstances – that almost always relate to human intervention.

Aluminum serves no biological function in the human body, yet can impair hundreds of processes. Aluminum is a known neurotoxin that can readily interfere with DNA.

You might find conflicting stories – but the long and the short of it is that there is no known biological function for aluminum. In fact quite the opposite – it is well known that aluminum can interfere with a whole host of systems in the human body – that's why it is limited in amounts by the FDA in many medical products – and there are safety limits set on how much you can receive in IV products.

For infants – the FDA sets limits of 25 mcg per day for an infant who is IV fed – because otherwise it can reach toxic amounts over time. Here is the letter outlining this by the FDA: https://www.fda.gov/ohrms/dockets/98fr/oc0367.pdf

So here's the thing – if we know aluminum is toxic enough to need to limit the exposure to – then there is obviously a potential for toxicity. A simple search anywhere on Google, Google Scholar, or PubMed will yield thousands and thousands of results – so there really isn't any need for me to drum on and on about it anymore – you can very easily verify this by going to look yourself. It won't take you long to find more studies than you need.

So here becomes the problem:

If the FDA has imposed limits of 25 mcg per day of aluminum due to potential toxicity, how much sense does the current CDC schedule make that drastically exceeds the limits set on other IV products? Let's break it down:

Using the 5 mcg/kg/day criterion from the first document as a minimum amount we know a healthy baby could handle, a 12-pound 2-month-old baby could safely get at least 30 micrograms of aluminum in one day. A 22-pound one-year-old could get at least 50 micrograms safely. Babies with healthy kidneys could probably handle a lot more than this, but we at least know they could handle this amount.

However, these documents don't tell us what the maximum safe dose would be for a health baby or child. And I can't find such information anywhere. This is probably why the A.S.P.E.N. group suggests, and the FDA requires, that all injectable solutions have the 25 mcg limit, since we at least know that is safe.

According to the link I just posted, if premature babies get more than 10 micrograms of aluminum per day in their IV solution, this aluminum may accumulate in their bones and their brain in toxic levels. They also warn that toxicity is difficult to detect just by observing symptoms.

So let's take a look at the current schedule and some common vaccines:

- Hib (PedVaxHib brand only) – 225 micrograms per shot.
- Hepatitis B – 250 micrograms.

- DTaP – depending on the manufacturer, ranges from 170 to 625 micrograms.
- Pneumococcus – 125 micrograms.
- Hepatitis A – 250 micrograms.
- HPV – 225 micrograms.
- Pentacel (DTaP, HIB and Polio combo vaccine) – 330 micrograms.
- Pediarix (DTaP, Hep B and Polio combo vaccine) – 850 micrograms.

So – a newborn who gets a hepatitis B injection on day one of life would get 250 micrograms of aluminum. This would be repeated at one month of age with the next hepatitis B shot.

When a baby gets the first big round of shots at 2 months, the total dose of aluminum can vary from 295 micrograms (if a non-aluminum HIB and the lowest aluminum brand of DTaP is used) to a massive 1225 micrograms if the highest aluminum brands are used and Hep B vaccine is also given.

If these doses are repeated at 4 and 6 months. A child would continue to get some aluminum throughout the first 2 years with most rounds of shots.

Here's the next problem – these numbers don't even reflect the full advised schedule of the CDC.

Here is part of the schedule and amounts of aluminum here:

Birth: 74 mcg/kg (250 mcg for 3.4 kg infant) (Hep B only)
2 month: 245 mcg/kg (1225 mcg for 5 kg infant) (Hep B, DTaP, HiB, pneumococcal, polio)
4 month: 150 mcg/kg (975 mcg for 6.5 kg infant) (DTaP, HiB, and pneumococcal)

6 month: 153 mcg/kg (1225 mcg for 8 kg infant) (Hep B, DTaP, HiB, pneumococcal, polio)

So upon looking at this – one has to question the sanity of such recommendations.

We're not talking exceeding the amounts by just a little bit – we're talking exceeding the amounts by 50 times or more. That means if you follow the full CDC schedule – you'd be giving in a single sitting an amount of aluminum that exceeds the FDA-set limits for any other medication or treatment by 50 times or more.

That's the same as sitting your infant down and putting 50 days' worth of a product with an aluminum limit – and giving them all 50 days at once.

Now that we've established that potential problem – let's go back to the article I listed in the section on "Fluoride" that was straight from the FDA – that fluoride exponentially increases the toxicity of all heavy metals – including aluminum.

Many doctors have speculated that this is possibly part of why America has a much higher rate of autism than every other country in the world – because America is one of the only countries to force-fluoridate their water supply.

I'd just like to point out – the FDA and other regulatory agencies were forced to drop fluoride levels in many areas due to it causing dental fluorosis – a sign that people are getting too much fluoride.
https://www.theguardian.com/environment/2015/apr/27/fluoride-levels-us-drinking-water-lowered-splotchy-teeth

You can find more links all across the Internet as well as the back of the book in the section on fluoride.

So – both fluoride and aluminum are nephrotoxic and tax the kidneys. Together they have a synergistic toxicity as well – making them far more toxic than either on its own.

This is just the tip of the iceberg on this subject – I suggest reading some of the studies on aluminum.

Vaccines and SIDS

Every vaccine insert lists death as a possible outcome from vaccines. Rather than make this exceptionally long winded – I suggest that you simply read this exceptionally well put-together article from Dr. Kelly Brogan.

To attempt to write it better (or even as well as her) would be pointless since she does such a great job, so I encourage you to head over here to read it:
http://kellybroganmd.com/driving-epidemic-sudden-infant-death-sids/

Remember – the United States has the highest infant mortality rate of any first world country – and even higher than some second world countries. Your job as a parent is to ask why, and I feel that Dr. Kelly Brogan does a really great job of pointing a few things out that are very concerning. There will also be more studies highlighting the same thing at the end of the book.

There is also the graph from GlaxoSmithKline themselves who claim there is "no link" to their vaccine and SIDS – which you may review for yourself here (next page):

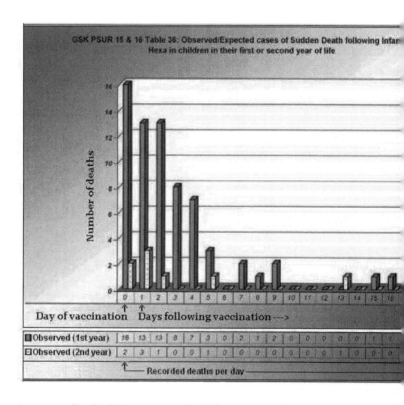

GSK PSUR 15 & 16 Table 36: Observed/Expected cases of Sudden Death following Infanr Hexa in children in their first or second year of life

	0	1	2	3	4	5	6	7	8	9	10	11	12	13	14	15	16
Observed (1st year)	16	13	13	8	7	3	0	2	1	2	0	0	0	0	0	1	1
Observed (2nd year)	2	3	1	0	0	1	0	0	0	0	0	0	0	1	0	0	0

Day of vaccination   Days following vaccination --->

Recorded deaths per day

I personally think GSK must think I'm an idiot if they want me to believe that this is "coincidence".

A study finding similar results to the previous facts may be found here:

Infant mortality rates regressed against number of vaccine doses routinely given: Is there a biochemical or synergistic toxicity?

https://www.ncbi.nlm.nih.gov/pmc/articles/PMC3170075/

Also finally – here is one study showing that those who received the DTaP vaccine were 5 times more likely to die than those who received no vaccine. Unfortunately this is one of the very few studies that have ever been done like this:
https://www.ncbi.nlm.nih.gov/pmc/articles/PMC5360569/pdf/main.pdf

"There is no proof that vaccines can cause autism"

That is the current medical consensus and the stance held by the FDA and the CDC.

I however here – will just put a hundred links or so up to studies that link vaccines and autism. You're welcome to start reading them. It's not necessary – I'm merely putting them here to show that the studies DO indeed exist – and it's a lot more than the ones used by the FDA and the CDC to claim there is no link. They use 4 or 5 – I give you a hundred saying it's possible. You draw your own conclusion on if it's possible there just might be a link or not. I know where I stand. Just check the back of the book for the list of studies that show that vaccines can and most certainly do contribute to autism. There's a LOT of them so we put them back there.

"The science is settled"

This is the dumbest statement that anyone could ever utter. I don't like to be derogatory – but in this case it warrants it.

There is absolutely no such thing as "settled science" – ever. To imply that there is would mean we know absolutely everything about a given topic – down to exactly how "quantum physics" or whatever the new science is at the time works completely.

Only someone incredibly arrogant would utter such a statement as a defense of an opinion.

My best advice – anyone who uses that statement should just be avoided – because nothing you say or do will change their mind. They've completely given up on even entertaining the idea or hearing what you have to say – let alone trying to get them to actually read any studies.

Just avoid these people.

Financial Compensation for Vaccination

Many pediatricians maintain the stance that they make no money from giving vaccines to your child. However currently Blue Cross Blue Shield gives a 400-dollar bonus for every child that is fully vaccinated by age 2 (including the flu shot) – but **ONLY** if 63% or more of their patients are fully vaccinated that year.

Given that a pediatric clinic may see 200 or more patients:

$400 x 200 = $80,000 that might be on the line if your child is the one that would cause their numbers to drop below 60% - something that people argue might cause a pediatrician to give shots to somebody who shouldn't necessarily be getting them or need them.

There might be other insurance company payouts as well – unfortunately the majority of these compensations are unknown to me and change fairly frequently. Be sure to do your digging if you want to know the answers to these questions.

"Vaccines saved us from infectious diseases"

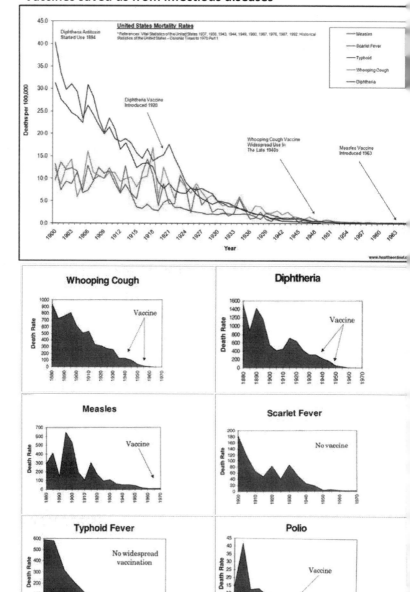

I'm not using these graphs to say that vaccines don't work or that they are worthless – I'm merely pointing out that nearly nobody died from these illness before the release of the vaccine (at the time of release anyhow). So we can state from these that vaccines had little to no impact on mortality rates from said infected diseases.

Perhaps quarantine, sanitation systems, and clean water halted the spread of diseases – and improved nutrition after the Great Depression lowered the death rate.

Once again – I'm not pointing this out to say that vaccines do not work or that they are unnecessary – I'm pointing out the effect vaccines had on the death rate of said diseases when they were introduced. This book is about education – not telling you what to do – or to discourage you from vaccinating. It's simply to help you make the best decision for yourself.

Andrew Wakefield

This topic is very long and I won't go into it in detail because it's better to just look into the topic yourself – and even better hear it from him personally on the movie "Vaxxed" in the "Behind the Scenes" part.

There are multiple sources saying he has been exonerated, and some saying he still hasn't been. The problem is it's tough to say – that's why I included the recommendation to the movie "Vaxxed" and listen to him tell about what happened.

I will however put this out there – the same study that was "falsified" and used to take his license away – had at least 10 other authors that signed off on the paper – and all of them suffered no consequence.

--

So – one has to ask the question how only 1 of 10 or more doctors loses their license over a study when they all signed off on it.

One more thing to read about (and this study will be quoted again later):

"The average MMR coverage for the three countries fell below 90% after Dr. Wakefield's infamous 1998 publication but started to recover slowly after 2001 until reaching over 90% coverage again by 2004. During the same time period, the average autism spectrum disorder prevalence in the United Kingdom, Norway and Sweden dropped substantially after birth year 1998 and gradually increased again after birth year 2000.

"Vaccines manufactured in human fetal cell lines contain unacceptably high levels of fetal DNA fragment contaminants. The human genome naturally contains regions that are susceptible to double strand break formation and DNA insertional mutagenesis. The 'Wakefield Scare' created a natural experiment that may demonstrate a causal relationship between fetal cell-line manufactured vaccines and ASD prevalence."

https://www.ncbi.nlm.nih.gov/m/pubmed/26103708/

It should be noted that at no other time in recent history has the rate of autism regressed since the early 1990s – making this study even more compelling to think about.

This study from the Mayo Clinic is also interesting – as Dr. Wakefield pointed out that African American children were the ones who were especially vulnerable to the MMR vaccine when it came to autism:

"Somali Americans develop twice the antibody response to rubella from the current vaccine compared to Caucasians in a new Mayo Clinic study on individualized aspects of immune response. A non-Somali, African-American cohort ranked next in immune response, still significantly higher than Caucasians, and Hispanic Americans in the study were least responsive to the vaccine. The findings appear in the journal *Vaccine*."

http://newsnetwork.mayoclinic.org/discussion/mayo-clinic-discovers-african-americans-respond-better-to-rubella-vaccine/

It should also be noted that Somalians living in America have the highest rates of autism of any ethnicity. Also – before coming to America – Somalians didn't even have a word for "autism" because it didn't exist.

What also is extremely interesting – is loads of people know who Andrew Wakefield is – and his alleged fraud.

Yet – no one seems to know anything about a man named Poul Thorsen – and individual contracted by the CDC to vaccine safety studies – and was convicted of multiple counts of money laundering, fraud, and more. You may read just a snippet about this man here: http://www.ageofautism.com/2016/02/dr-poul-thorsen-stil-funded-while-on-fugitive-list.html
Yes, I understand that this is not exactly a "reliable link" – it just has really good links to actual good sources within the page – so that is why I used that link. You can also do independent research on him (and are encouraged to do so).

I'm just pointing out here how well our mainstream media controls a narrative – and how it's interesting a lead researcher of the CDC guilty of multiple felonies somehow goes unnoticed by so many people somehow. It's almost like pharmaceutical companies – who pay the majority of advertising on TV and in publications – have an ability to "sway" what information gets covered. Unless of course a thing like that would never happen…

Like I said – do some digging yourself. Ask questions.

MTHFR

MTHFR is a genetic mutation caused by RoundUp in where the active synthetic amino acid replaces the Glycine in DNA – disabling detoxification mechanisms and making people unable to methylate certain substances. In essence, this makes people more susceptible to vaccine damage and less able to detoxify from vaccines. The entire congressional hearing on the topic of RoundUp can be found on the website https://www.stayhealthymyfriends.win/mthfr. I would suggest looking at it – especially **Sterling Hill's** presentation.

Also included are the results from independently tested vaccines – finding many contained the weed-killer RoundUp – from the tainted/polluted gelatin used in them. The highest levels were found in the MMR vaccine – the same vaccine that Andrew Wakefield wrote his paper on disrupted gut health after vaccination and its relation to autism. RoundUp is well known to disrupt the microbiome drastically in human gut (as well as transfer DNA between the promiscuous gram-positive bacteria there). I'm just throwing this out there for you to draw your own conclusion on. Not saying there's a link – however I'm not saying there's not.

I will however say – that **I personally talked to the FDA in April of 2017 – and they were well aware of the studies of RoundUp contaminating vaccines.**

They assured me that they were not – however **when I asked if they had done even one single test or had even one test that they could give me to prove it – they said "no because it would be too expensive"**.

Well.....a private citizen managed to afford to do it – so....draw your own conclusions. Call the FDA yourself and ask for any proof that vaccines do not contain RoundUp.

It should also be noted that there are absolutely no studies showing what the safe level of the weed-killer RoundUp is if injected into a human or animal. It could be a lot – it could be a miniscule amount – we have no idea because there are no official studies (however I'm sure Monsanto is hard at work on producing some favorable studies and lobbying Congress/doctors/researchers to get one).

Mitochondrial disorders

Mitochondrial disorders are a well known issue when it comes to vaccines in the natural health community – and the mainstream medical community is starting to catch on. Due to rampant mycoplasma infections (I suggest people watch the YouTube video from Garth Nicolson on weaponized mycoplasmas) and Lyme's disease – any person having either of these two things has their mitochondria and detoxification abilities severely lowered. Garth Nicolson also points out in his videos that nearly all of the vaccines have been contaminated with mycoplasmas and are impossible to fully remove. Also – due to (explained more in the next section) the aborted fetal cell lines being contaminated with retroviruses and mycoplasmas that are impossible to clean – these make their way into vaccines as well.

Aborted Fetal Tissue

About 50% of the vaccines on the market contain aborted fetal tissue – because the viruses in the "live virus vaccines" (yes there are live viruses in vaccines that are supposed to be deactivated or weakened) are grown in aborted fetal tissue. One of the independent tests done on vaccines found the levels of aborted fetal DNA to be 1000x higher than was FDA allowed.

Also concerning in this topic – is that there have been no tests done to show what the effects are of injecting every baby in the United States with both male – and female – DNA. Last I checked – DNA was self replicating – meaning a little bit can turn into a lot. Do we know how this affects the people injected over time? No – because those studies have never been done. Do we know what this does to a person's sense of identity or sexuality (such as a male being injected with female DNA)? No – because those studies have never been done.

With the recent and emerging field of epigenetics and the ability for memories to be passed through DNA – one would have to ponder how much of the trauma of being aborted is carried in the DNA of said fetus used to make the vaccine? How much gets integrated into someone else's DNA? These studies have barely even been thought of – let alone been done. So you will have to weigh that option for yourself and see if you want to inject your child with the DNA from aborted fetuses from both sexes over and over.

Here are a few studies that I do really want to link and quote for you:

Epidemiologic and Molecular Relationship Between Vaccine Manufacture and Autism Spectrum Disorder Prevalence

"The average MMR coverage for the three countries fell below 90% after Dr. Wakefield's infamous 1998 publication but started to recover slowly after 2001 until reaching over 90% coverage again by 2004. During the same time period, the average autism spectrum disorder prevalence in the United Kingdom, Norway and Sweden dropped substantially after birth year 1998 and gradually increased again after birth year 2000.

"Vaccines manufactured in human fetal cell lines contain unacceptably high levels of fetal DNA fragment contaminants. The human genome naturally contains regions that are susceptible to double strand break formation and DNA insertional mutagenesis. The 'Wakefield Scare' created a natural experiment that may demonstrate a causal relationship between fetal cell-line manufactured vaccines and ASD prevalence."

https://www.ncbi.nlm.nih.gov/m/pubmed/26103708/

Spontaneous Integration of Human DNA Fragments into Host Genome

"Not only damaged human cells, but also healthy human cells can take up foreign DNA spontaneously. Foreign human DNA taken up by human cells will be transported into nuclei and be integrated into host genome, which will cause phenotype change. Hence, residual human fetal DNA fragments in vaccine can be one of causes of autism spectrum disorder in children through vaccination. Vaccine must be safe without any human DNA contaminations or reactivated viruses, and must be produced in ethically approved manufacturing processes."

http://soundchoice.org/wp-content/uploads/2012/08/DNA_Contaminants_in_Vaccines_Can_Integrate_Into_Childrens_Genes.pdf

I have my thoughts on this issue.

Also here becomes another predicament – the FDA and vaccine manufacturers know that the DNA from aborted fetal cells gets into vaccines. Their solution was to break the DNA down more in an attempt to solve this problem – but instead made the problem worse. When it was broken down into smaller pieces – it made it easier for it to enter the cell of the host and get taken up by that cell and the host.

Now – couple that with the aluminum that inhibits DNA replication – you're not only silencing normal DNA replication in healthy cells – you're also introducing foreign DNA in as well that can further mutate the process.

Couple that with the fact that these DNA fragments are being introduced into rapidly dividing cells – this makes it much worse than an adult being injected with DNA from other people – because the DNA that has been uptaken by the host now replicates rapidly inside of these cells due to their fast replication.

In other words – people who have injected their kids with vaccines that contain aborted fetal DNA – aren't really raising their kids any more. Their raising their kids and the other kids who's DNA is inside them.

I don't have any proof of this – but one could certainly speculate that this could lead to the gender identity crisis that our country appears to have today (among many other things yes – but this is one we certainly can't rule out as no studies exist to prove this is safe in any way shape or form. Actually – they exist proving that it's NOT safe).

Acetaminophen (Tylenol) and Vaccination

This topic is pretty blunt – because well – it has to be.

If your doctor recommends Tylenol after a vaccine to reduce a fever – kindly reeducate them on this topic. "Kindly" is the key word here. Get them a copy of this study to read over – specifically the part on Tylenol:
http://journals.sagepub.com/doi/pdf/10.1177/0300060517693423 UK. Tylenol = Paracetamol.

For the rest of us lay-folk – what has been found is that Tylenol drastically lowers glutathione levels when used. It is also the #1 cause of liver failure in the UK. Glutathione is what is known as the "mother of all antioxidants" and is produced in the liver (through a very long and complicated process indeed). Studies find (many of them) that taking Tylenol after a vaccination not only lowers the response to the vaccine – but drastically increases the risk of having an adverse reaction.

To illustrate this point – it is well known in Cuba that this is something to avoid at all costs – and they have an autism rate of 1 in 60,000 as of 2011. The United States is up to 1 in 33 in some places (possibly more by the time you read this) – but was at 1 in 91 during the time that Cuba was at 1 in 60,000.

I highly doubt that "better diagnostic criteria" could possibly account for such a difference.

"The current CDC schedule for vaccinations are safe"

No studies have ever been done to prove that the current vaccine schedule is safe.

You can go see the congressional testimony to this on YouTube if you want to watch the head of the CDC admit it herself as of the writing of this book.

I won't spend much time here because this is pretty straightforward. There are no studies – and there is a video of the head of the CDC admitting it in a congressional hearing. Not much to argue here.

"giving more than one vaccine at one time is safe"

There has been only one study on giving more than one vaccine at once and whether it is safe or not – except this second one that was originally published in the American Journal of Pediatrics in April 2016:
http://www.jpands.org/vol21no2/miller.pdf

"Summary of Results and Media Response Our study showed that infants who receive several vaccines concurrently, as recommended by CDC, are significantly more likely to be hospitalized or die when compared with infants who receive fewer vaccines simultaneously. It also showed that reported adverse effects were more likely to lead to hospitalization or death in younger infants.

"These findings are so troubling that we expected major media outlets in America to sound an alarm, calling for an immediate reevaluation of current preventive health care practices. But 4 years after publication of our study, this has not happened."

Could it be because, according to Robert Kennedy, Jr., about 70% of advertising revenue on network news comes from drug companies? In fact, the president of a network news division admitted that he would fire a host who brought on a guest that led to loss of a pharmaceutical account. That may be why the mainstream media won't give equal time to stories about problems with vaccine safety.

Conclusion

The safety of CDC's childhood vaccination schedule was never affirmed in clinical studies. Vaccines are administered to millions of infants every year, yet health authorities have no scientific data from synergistic toxicity studies on all combinations of vaccines that infants are likely to receive.

National vaccination campaigns must be supported by scientific evidence. No child should be subjected to a health policy that is not based on sound scientific principles and, in fact, has been shown to be potentially dangerous.

"Undesirable outcomes associated with childhood vaccination can be reduced by requiring national vaccination policies to be supported by scientific evidence, holding vaccine manufacturers accountable when their products harm consumers, and urging major news outlets that rely on pharmaceutical advertising revenue to change their business models so that crucial scientific research, regardless of how controversial it may be, is widely disseminated into the public domain. Meanwhile, the evidence presented in this study shows that multiple vaccines administered during one visit, and vaccinating young infants, significantly increase morbidity and mortality."

"Parents and physicians should consider health options associated with a lower risk of hospitalization or death."

While the CDC claims that giving more than one vaccine at a time is safe – they provide no studies to prove so:
https://www.cdc.gov/vaccinesafety/concerns/multiple-vaccines-immunity.html

I actually emailed the CDC and after about a week they did respond citing me studies that they used to justify that giving up to 8 vaccines at once or 21 vaccines in a month is safe.

Every single article was either redacted, has a sample size of under 150 people, is 30 or 40 years old, or includes the use of the Oral Polio Vaccine in the study (ask India how this turned out or why we no longer use the OPV). In most cases multiple of these statements were true.

They did include one study from the infamous "Paul Offit" (more on him later) in which he states "**an infant could theoretically handle 10,000 vaccines at once**". He uses no actual studies – but argues that the number of antigens in one vaccine is small so an infant could theoretically handle 10,000 at once. I'll be square here – this guy is not someone that as a parent I trust.

Also the CDC's studies they use to justify the "safety" of giving multiple vaccines at once – is not something that gives me much reassurance as a parent either. You may always email the CDC for these studies and look them over yourself.

"Vaccinated children are healthier than non-vaccinated children"

No studies have been done to show this. In fact – the contrary has been shown: http://www.ebiomedicine.com/article/S2352-3964(17)30046-4/fulltext

"DTP was associated with 5-fold higher mortality than being unvaccinated. No prospective study has shown beneficial survival effects of DTP. Unfortunately, DTP is the most widely used vaccine, and the proportion who receives DTP3 is used globally as an indicator of the performance of national vaccination programs.

"It should be of concern that the effect of routine vaccinations on all-cause mortality was not tested in randomized trials. All

DTP = Diphtheria Tetanus Pertussis (whooping cough)

94

currently available evidence suggests that DTP vaccine may kill more children from other causes than it saves from diphtheria, tetanus or pertussis. Though a vaccine protects children against the target disease it may simultaneously increase susceptibility to unrelated infections.

"The recently published SAGE review called for randomized trials of DTP (Higgins et al., 2014). However, at the same time the IVIR-AC committee to which SAGE delegated the follow-up studies of the NSEs of vaccines has indicated that it will not be possible to examine the effect of DTP in an unbiased way. If that decision by IVIR-AC remains unchallenged, the present study may remain the closest we will ever come to a RCT of the NSEs of DTP."

It should also be noted that recipients of the DTaP vaccine can become asymptomatic carriers and spread it to other people.

Here is a video of one doctor with a Master's Degree in Business, Early Childhood, and more that clearly explains why he stopped vaccinating his patients and discourages parents from doing so – even though it costs him hundreds and hundreds of thousands of dollars every year. He also explains how the children he sees become autistic were "most certainly not always autistic" – using his masters in early childhood to draw his conclusion upon:

https://www.youtube.com/watch?v=UiJRUdY9I3E

"Everyone needs to get vaccinated to maintain herd immunity"

Unfortunately – we used to think this to be true – because we used to think vaccines gave lifetime immunity. In the past decade however – we've found that vaccine immunity wanes over time. In cases such as the DTaP – it was found that antibody response dropped to only 43% in the course of only one year!

What this means is that we have never even come close to "herd immunity" – because every adult would need to get a booster shot for every single disease nearly every year.

So if your pediatrician that you asked if they would be comfortable taking the CDC's current vaccine schedule replied they "didn't need it" – on the contrary – they should be the first people lining up to make sure they are "up to date" with all their immunizations due to all the children they see on a daily basis.

A longer article on this outlines it beautifully here: https://medium.com/@jbhandley/the-medical-time-bomb-of-immunization-against-disease-faa9eefa87e2

"It would be unethical to do a vaccinated vs. unvaccinated study"

This statement is one that the CDC has used for decades to avoid doing such a study.

I ask you:

What would be unethical about going through medical records – selecting vaccinated vs. unvaccinated (because we know

about 3% of kids are unvaccinated and who they are) and selecting "rates of autism, allergies, eczema, learning disabilities, IEPs, cancer rates, SIDS rates, and so forth" – then comparing the data?

Over 700 companies have access to this data as of now – what is stopping them from doing that? Is this even a hard concept? What harm could possibly come from doing such a study? What about that would be unethical in any way? Would it even be remotely difficult?

I have my opinions on why this hasn't been done – you are welcome to draw your own.

Additionally – vaccine manufacturers are immune to any and all lawsuits concerning their product – no matter how poorly they are manufactured.

In 1986 vaccine manufacturers were given legal immunity because they were receiving too many lawsuits – and threatened to stop making vaccines. Congress then passed the "National Childhood Vaccine Injury Act" – giving them complete immunity from vaccine-related lawsuits.

Additionally – a special "vaccine court" was set up where parents then had to go up against the U.S. Government in court – instead of the manufacturer of the vaccine. Also – all payouts from injuries are paid by a tax on vaccines and by the U.S. taxpayer (every vaccine has a $0.75 tax on it to help cover lawsuits).

Currently the vaccine court has paid out over 3.6 billion dollars in damages. People also argue that since there are what are called "Special Masters" instead of elected judges – that the numbers may be well off what the actual representation is. Many times families go through years of court proceedings (while trying to care for a vaccine-injured child) and end up going too broke to continue on the trial – another point that people argue is skewing the data.

I would read this article as well describing what a nightmare the immunity to lawsuits is: http://articles.mercola.com/sites/articles/archive/2017/04/11/big-pharma-immunity-against-vaccines-lawsuits.aspx

Also – since the convenient immunity to lawsuits – pharmaceutical companies have very little incentive to recall vaccines that aren't exactly manufactured the best – such as this one where the company knew there were shards of glass in the vaccine – but didn't feel it was worth recalling them: http://www.thelibertybeacon.com/no-recall-glass-found-vaccines-made-monroe-county/

Asking for independent testing to ensure vaccines are not contaminated with foreign materials

I find it best to just quote an article here:

Every Human Vaccine Tested Was Contaminated by Unsafe Levels of Metals and Debris Linked to Cancer and Autoimmune Disease, New Study Reports

.

Researchers examining 44 samples of 30 different vaccines found dangerous contaminants, including red blood cells in one vaccine and metal toxicants in every single sample tested – except in one animal vaccine.

Using extremely sensitive new technologies not used in vaccine manufacturing, Italian scientists reported they were "baffled" by their discoveries which included single particles and aggregates of organic debris including red cells of human or possibly animal origin and metals including lead, tungsten, gold, and chromium, that have been linked to autoimmune disease and leukemia.

In the study - (http://medcraveonline.com/IJVV/IJVV-04-00072.pdf), published in the *International Journal of Vaccines and Vaccination*, the researchers led by Antonietta Gatti, of the National Council of Research of Italy and the Scientific Director of Nanodiagnostics, say their results "show the presence of micro- and nano-sized particulate matter composed of inorganic elements in vaccine samples" not declared in the products' ingredients lists.

Lead particles were found in the cervical cancer vaccines, Gardasil and Cervarix, for example, and in the seasonal flu vaccine Aggripal manufactured by Novartis as well as in the Meningetec vaccine meant to protect against meningitis C.

Samples of an infant vaccine called Infarix Hexa (against diphtheria, tetanus, pertussis, hepatitis B, poliomyelitis and haemophilus influenzae type B) manufactured by GlaxoSmithKline was found to contain stainless steel, tungsten and a gold-zinc aggregate.

Other metal contaminants included platinum, silver, bismuth, iron, and chromium. Chromium (alone or in alloy with iron and nickel) was identified in 25 of the human vaccines from Italy and France that were tested.

GSK's Fluarix vaccine for children three years and older contained 11 metals and aggregates of metals. Similar aggregates to those identified in the vaccines have been shown to be prevalent in cases of leukemia (https://www.ncbi.nlm.nih.gov/pubmed/27669365), the researchers noted.

Many of the vaccines contained iron and iron alloys which, according to the researchers, "can corrode (https://www.ncbi.nlm.nih.gov/pubmed/8077264) and the corrosion products (https://www.ncbi.nlm.nih.gov/pubmed/9066525) exert a toxicity affecting the tissues".

The researchers supply an image of an area in a drop of Sanofi Pasteur MSD's Repevax (diphtheria, pertussis, tetanus, polio) vaccine "where the morphology of red cells – we cannot tell whether they are human or animal – is clearly visible" along with the presence of "debris" composed of aluminum, bromine, silicon, potassium and titanium.

Feligen, the only veterinary vaccine tested in the 44 total vaccines sampled, proved to be the only sample free from inorganic contamination.

No studies have been done on the synergistic toxicity of all of these different materials – but it should be noted that synergistic toxicity can very rapidly raise toxicity levels – even with only small amounts present.

This is why I ask you to acquire independent testing – because there are more studies like this that have found the same thing. As I state in the "immunity to lawsuits" section – there is nothing anyone can do except try to prove to the U.S. Government that these dirty vaccines caused an adverse event – something that would probably be exceptionally difficult to do.

Vaccines may well be causing the explosion of auto-immune epidemics

The immune system is a highly complicated system that we are still not even close to fully understanding. If we did – our country would not be as sick as it is.

The basis of this claim is well explained by many doctors. By continually bypassing the humoral immune system and stimulating only half of the immune system – we are overly and continually pushing the immune system in one direction and artificially stimulating it to active in only TH2 immune response – which can cause the body's immune system to start attacking itself due to overstimulation.

Watch this 5-minute video from a doctor explaining it very simply:
https://www.youtube.com/watch?v=n0e6I9qHSCl

The other problem is – the part of the immune system that we are trying to stimulate with vaccines, represents only 2% of the immune system.

Included in every vaccine insert:

"This product has not been evaluated for carcinogenic or mutagenic properties"

This is stated in each and every vaccine insert. Ask your doctor to read them for you and find it (or look it up on your own – there will also be copies in this book).

Here's the problem – every vaccine contains ingredients that are known carcinogens.

1. Acetone: This clear, volatile liquid is used as a paint solvent and nail polish remover. It is also well known as an industrial chemical used in plastics and manufacturing.
2. Aluminum phosphate and aluminum sulfate: Known also by its chemical makeup, phosphoric acid and aluminum salt, aluminum phosphate consists of a corrosive acid and neurotoxin. Similarly, aluminum sulfate is known by its components, sulfuric acid, an extremely carcinogenic and corrosive acid, and aluminum salt, a neurotoxin.
3. Benzethonium chloride: This dangerous chemical is a known carcinogen. It is also known to cause genetic mutations in unborn children.
4. Ethanol: Also known as ethyl alcohol, ethanol is known to cause vomiting, headaches, drowsiness, and unconsciousness.
5. Formaldehyde: This is an extremely dangerous carcinogen, as well as a source of genetic mutation in the unborn.
6. Glutaraldehyde: This liquid chemical has a number of industrial uses, including use as a disinfectant, preservative, biocide, hardening agent, and embalming agent. It is known to cause <u>asthma</u>, allergies, breathing problems, and coughing.

7. Human serum albumin: A human protein, but it can only be broken down when digested. When it is injected it can cause autoimmune encephalitis (AE) disorders and <u>allergies</u>.

8. Animal components: Vaccines contain both monkey cells, which carry viruses that can cause cancer and diseases, as well as baby cow blood after the red blood cells have been removed. The latter, known as calf serum, can be extremely contaminated with viruses and bacteria. Researchers have recently linked contaminated vaccines to be the cause of many Hand, Foot, and Mouth (coxsackievirus) outbreaks.

9. Polysorbate 80: This chemical is an emulsifier and a surfactant known to cause infertility. Polysorbate 80 is also known to increase the risk of stroke and <u>heart attack</u>.

10. Phenol-carbolic acid: This corrosive acid has been identified by the Centers for Disease Control and Prevention as an extremely hazardous substance. The CDC itself recommends avoiding all contact. The chemical is known to cause a host of symptoms, from nausea, vomiting, and dizziness to the more serious symptoms of convulsions, coma, and even death.

11. Thimerosal: Also known as ethylmercury, thimerosal is 49.6 percent mercury, the second most toxic element on earth next to plutonium.
And, yes, this too is a known neurotoxin.

This is not a complete list – but paints the picture of how there are indeed cancer-causing ingredients in vaccines.

However, people will argue that they are only in vaccines in very small amounts. This is true. However – we have no idea what the effects are on injected formaldehyde vs. oral or inhaled are – because these studies have never been done. So while their argument of "It's only a small amount" is correct – the argument that when you inject something makes it exceptionally more toxic is also correct. You decide what your thoughts are on this.

Thimerosal

This topic is a rough one. Thimerosal is a mercury derivative, however, experts claim it is safe. Many claim it is not.

The CDC states that Thimerosal is safe – and links only between 4 and 6 studies saying so. However if you head over to www.pubmed.gov and type in "Thimerosal toxicity" you will find well over a hundred studies documenting its toxicity.

Thimerosal was removed from vaccines "just in case" (well not actually removed – but lowered to the point where they could call it Thimerosal-free) around 2002 after a backlash from something called the "Simpsonwood Meeting" – I would head to this link and read about it:
http://www.putchildrenfirst.org/chapter2.html

Essentially – people argue that the CDC doctored data by including children that were as young as 6 months of age to skew the data – since autism diagnosis doesn't happen usually until 18 – 24 months.

Also before its approval around 1930 – there was only one study done on the safety of Thimerosal. They tested it intravenously on 22 patients who had meningitis –

Every single one of them died.

Now do we know what they died from? No. However – that was the only study used to justify its use for decades.

I have my thoughts on if that's a safe clinical trial to license something – but you draw your own conclusions.

I also encourage readers to take a look at this study:

Thimerosal-Derived Ethylmercury Is a Mitochondrial Toxin in Human Astrocytes: Possible Role of Fenton Chemistry in the Oxidation and Breakage of mtDNA

https://www.hindawi.com/journals/jt/2012/373678/

I'm no rocket scientist – but pretty sure that this spells it out really clearly that Thimerosal isn't safe by any means. But seriously folks – I'm just getting started on this topic.

Just for fun take a look at this study too on how Thimerosal is causing problems in contact lens solution:
https://www.ncbi.nlm.nih.gov/pubmed/6810487

So – people can be allergic to mercury (Thimerosal) you say? That is probably something people should be tested for before they get injected with a Thimerosal containing vaccine. Also – be aware the RhoGam shot also contains Thimerosal still – but that is covered in a different chapter of this book. Just worth mentioning while we're talking Thimerosal.

Finally here is one more link that contains a series of slides on the differences between ethylmercury and methylmercury for those that want to educate themselves. This is one I REALLY hope people take a quick peek at:
http://www.whale.to/a/comparative_toxicity_of_ethyl.html

Finally here is just one study that shows that Thimerosal is quite certainly linked to autism:

A two-phase study evaluating the relationship between Thimerosal-containing vaccine administration and the risk for an autism spectrum disorder diagnosis in the United States
https://www.ncbi.nlm.nih.gov/pmc/articles/PMC3878266/

On to the next part of the problem!

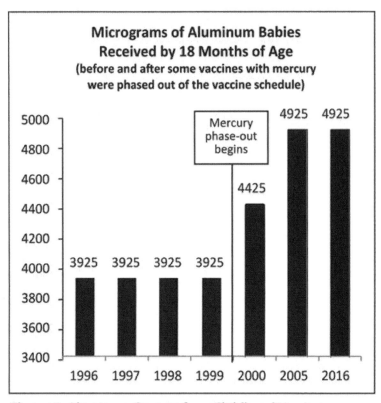

Micrograms of Aluminum Babies Received by 18 Months of Age
(before and after some vaccines with mercury were phased out of the vaccine schedule)

Figure 1. Aluminum Content from Childhood Vaccines

Vaccines containing aluminum were added to the childhood immunization schedule when some vaccines containing mercury were removed. Prior to the mercury phase-out (pre-2000), babies received 3,925 mcg of aluminum by 18 months of age. After pneumococcal and hepatitis A vaccines were added to the schedule, babies began receiving 4,925 mcg of aluminum during the same age period—a 25% increase.

Source: The vaccine manufacturers' product inserts and the CDC's annual childhood vaccination schedules.

Also – people make the argument that Thimerosal was removed from vaccines and yet autism rates remained unchanged. This is true (mostly, but not completely – depends on the vaccine. Also it should be noted that Thimerosal is not actually

COMPLETELY out of vaccines – it has just been lowered to a level that it doesn't have to be included in the ingredient list).

However – aluminum content in vaccines also was raised by 25% - and conveniently – the hepatitis B vaccine was moved to day 1 of a baby's life at the same time. This could completely skew the studies. Some people argue this was done on purpose to hide the drop in autism rates when Thimerosal was removed and skew the data. It's extremely tough to be sure – because very few people would actually know that answer – and one of them is not me. I have my opinions – but I can't tell you I know for sure. When we get to the hepatitis B vaccine segment soon – you may start to draw stronger opinions.

Also drawing upon the aluminum problem here – is this study in which aluminum is found to contribute to ALS: https://www.ncbi.nlm.nih.gov/pubmed/1467159 That's right – it too is a neurotoxin which we will describe later in this book. So – if it can cause ALS, what other neurological symptoms do you think it can cause?

A website I encountered also paints an interesting picture on Thimerosal, which is as follows. Remember – do not take just one thing into consideration when deciding if Thimerosal is safe or harmful – just put it into your "food for thought" area and weigh your decision carefully:

"Thimerosal is an organic compound that is 49.6 percent ethylmercury. Eli Lilly and Co., the Indianapolis-based drug giant, developed and registered thimerosal under its trade name Merthiolate in 1929 and began marketing it as an antibacterial, antifungal product. It became the most widely used preservative in vaccines. Thimerosal cannot be used with live-cell vaccines, such as MMR (measles, mumps, rubella) or polio, because it would kill the vaccine. The only research looking into the safety of thimerosal was done in 1930 by Eli Lilly-sponsored doctors, who injected it into 22 patients with meningitis. The human experiments failed to prove that thimerosal was nontoxic. Nonetheless, researchers H.M. Powell and W.A. Jamieson published a study in September 1931 in the *American Journal of Hygiene* that stated thimerosal had a "low order of toxicity" for humans, without mentioning that the human subjects were ill and subsequently died. Internal Lilly documents from the time, however, revealed that the company's researchers were worried about Merthiolate's "burning qualities" when used on the skin. By 1935, Eli Lilly's Jameison had further evidence of thimerosal's toxicity when he received a letter from a researcher who had injected it into dogs and saw severe local reactions, leading him to state: "Merthiolate is unsatisfactory as a preservative for serum intended for use on dogs.

"In the 70 years since thimerosal/Merthiolate was developed, the FDA never required Eli Lilly to conduct clinical studies of its safety, despite ample evidence of its toxicity and its highly allergic properties. In fact, the FDA today still refers to the 1931 Powell and Jameison study on its Web site as indication of the "safety and effectiveness" of thimerosal as a preservative. Thimerosal/Merthiolate was widely used in over-the-counter products, including ointments, eye drops, nasal sprays and contact lens solution. In 1998, the FDA finally banned Thimerosal for use in OTC products—18 years after it began a safety review of mercury-containing products. It took another year before the CDC and the FDA would ask manufacturers to remove thimerosal from childhood vaccines. Eli Lilly stopped making Merthiolate-containing products in the mid-'80s but still profits from licensing agreements with pharmaceutical companies around the world.

"Eli Lilly faces hundreds of civil lawsuits from parents who blame thimerosal for their autistic children. But the pharmaceutical giant has powerful friends in the White House and in Congress. The elder George Bush sat on Lilly's board of directors in the 1970s, and White House Budget Director Mitch Daniels was a Lilly executive. Lilly CEO Sidney Taurel was named by President George W. Bush to the Homeland Security Advisory Council. In November 2002, Congress passed a provision, tucked into a spending measure for homeland security, to indemnify Eli Lilly from lawsuits and require families to seek compensation through the federally funded Vaccine Injury Compensation Program. It was repealed in February 2003 after public outcry. Senate Majority Leader Bill Frist (R-Tenn.) still hopes to pass a similar bill. Congressional consideration for Eli Lilly makes sense: In the 2002 election cycle, the company gave more than $1.5 million to federal candidates, with three quarters to Republicans, making it the fourth-biggest giver in the pharmaceutical industry, according to the Center for Responsive Politics. In the current election cycle, the company already has given close to $230,000 (67 percent to Republicans) to federal candidates.

"Eli Lilly may be determined to avoid liability for thimerosal, but that doesn't mean it has abandoned children with neurological problems. This year, the FDA approved Straterra, a new Eli Lilly drug for the treatment of Attention Deficit Hyperactivity Disorder. The irony that Eli Lilly profits from damaged children is not lost on parent Robert Krakow: "When Eli Lilly is promoting Straterra on TV, saying up to 10 percent of children can be helped, you realize what we are up against."
http://inthesetimes.com/article/649/

To start off the vaccines – I want to paint an example of what happens when we don't ask questions. The first example will be the Zika virus:

Zika Virus Vaccine

(http://www.reduas.com.ar/wp-content/uploads/downloads/2016/02/Informe-Zika-de-Reduas_TRAD.pdf)

REPORT from Physicians of Argentina in the Crop-Sprayed Villages regarding Dengue-Zika, microcephaly, and mass-spraying with chemical poisons Main points:

1. Dengue epidemic in Brazil persists endemically (on an ongoing basis) due to the marginalisation and misery of millions of people, especially in Northeast Brazil. On top of that, Zika virus, a similar disease although more benign, is now spreading.

2. A dramatic increase of congenital malformations, especially microcephaly in newborns, was detected and quickly linked to the Zika virus by the Brazilian Ministry of Health. However, they fail to recognise that in the area where most sick persons live, a chemical larvicide producing malformations in mosquitoes has been applied for 18 months, and that this poison (pyroproxyfen) is applied by the State on drinking water used by the affected population.

3. Previous Zika epidemics did not cause birth defects in newborns, despite infecting 75% of the population in those countries. Also, in other countries such as Colombia there are no records of microcephaly; however, there are plenty of Zika cases.

3. The pyroproxyfen being used (as recommended by WHO) is manufactured by Sumimoto Chemical, a Japanese subsidiary of Monsanto.

4. Brazilian doctors (Abrasco) are claiming that the strategy of chemical control is contaminating the environment as well as people, that it is not decreasing the amount of mosquitoes, and

that this strategy is in fact a commercial manoeuvre from the chemical poisons industry, deeply integrated into Latin American ministries of health as well as WHO and PAHO.

5. Massive spreading using planes, as the governments of Mercosur are considering, is criminal, useless, and a political manoeuvre to simulate that actions are taken. The basis of the progress of the disease lies in inequality and poverty, and the best defense are community-based actions.

6. The last strategy deployed in Brazil, and which might be replicated in all our countries, is the use of GM mosquitoes – a total failure, except for the company supplying mosquitoes.

To simply sum it up:

By ignoring and not asking simple, common-sense questions – like how does no other country have a "shrunken head" Zika virus problem except Brazil, despite there being a very high number of confirmed cases in countries around the entire continent? – you'll note the fear and panic that was sold, **and how they started spraying a class of chemicals related to the very one that was causing the problems – over millions of people's heads – because they did not ask questions.**

Remember the CDC in a tizzy over this? I sure do – and I wonder how on earth they did not ask these common-sense questions before spreading the level of fear that they did.

I mean – airlines were literally hosing people with insecticide in enclosed areas – anyone think this might be a problem?

It should also be noted that this insecticide kills mosquitos by causing bodily and neurological deformations in the offspring of mosquitos. Does this sound familiar to anyone???

This topic is simple enough that this should suffice.

Hepatitis B Vaccine

Symptoms of hepatitis B disease include nausea, vomiting, fatigue, low grade fever, pain and swelling in joints, headache and cough that may occur one to two weeks before the onset of jaundice (yellowing of the skin) and enlargement and tenderness of the liver, which can last for three to four weeks. Fatigue can last up to a year. According to *Harrison's,* in cases of acute hepatitis B "most patients do not require hospital care" and "95 percent of patients have a favorable course and recover completely" with the case-fatality ratio being "very low (approximately 0.1 percent)."

The U.S. and western Europe have always had among the lowest rates of hepatitis B disease in the world (0.1% to 0.5% of the general population) compared to countries in the Far East and Africa, where the disease affects 5-20% or more of the population. According to *Guide to Clinical Preventive Services*, in the U.S. "the greatest reported incidence [of hepatitis B] occurs in adults aged 20-39" and "the number of cases peaked in 1985 and has shown a continuous gradual decline since that time." In 1991, there were 18,003 cases of hepatitis B reported in the U.S. out of a total U.S. population of 248 million. According to the October 31, 1997 *Morbidity and Mortality Weekly Report* published by the CDC, in 1996 there were 10,637 cases of hepatitis B reported in the U.S. with **279 cases reported in children under the age of 14** and the CDC stated that "Hepatitis B continues to decline in most states, primarily because of a decrease in the number of cases among injecting drug users and, to a lesser extent, among both homosexuals and heterosexuals of both sexes."

Even though hepatitis B is an adult disease, is not highly contagious, is not deadly for most who contract it, and is not in epidemic form in the U.S. (except among high risk groups such as IV drug addicts), in 1991 the Advisory Committee on Immunization Practices (ACIP) of the Centers for Disease Control (CDC) recommended that all infants be injected with the first dose of hepatitis B vaccine at birth before being discharged from the hospital newborn nursery.

A similar recommendation was also made by the Committee on Infectious Diseases of the American Academy of Pediatrics (AAP). This, despite the fact almost nothing is known about the health and integrity of an individual baby's immune and neurological systems at birth.

In 1991, media reports generated by the CDC used hepatitis B disease statistics that were not anchored in documented fact but are still used today to promote mass hepatitis B vaccination. Most of the inflated disease statistics originate with statements generated by the Centers for Disease Control. In the 1991 ACIP Recommendations calling for mass vaccination with hepatitis B vaccine published in the *Morbidity and Mortality Weekly Report,* the CDC states that there are an "estimated 1 million-1.25 million persons with chronic hepatitis B infection in the United States" and that "each year approximately 4,000-5,000 of these persons die from chronic liver disease" and that "an estimated 200,000-300,000 new [hepatitis B] infections occurred annually during the period 1980-1991." The CDC gives no scientific reference for this data other than the CDC.

Just one year before the government's call for mass vaccination, hepatitis B vaccine maker SmithKline Beecham in their 1990 hepatitis B vaccine product insert stated, "The CDC estimates that there are approximately 0.5 to 1.0 million chronic carriers of hepatitis B virus in the U.S. and that this pool of carriers grows by 2% to 3% (12,000 to 20,000 individuals) annually."

To encourage states to mandate use of hepatitis B vaccine by all children, federal health officials at the Centers for Disease Control give grants and other financial incentives to state health departments to reward them for promoting mass vaccination. Since 1965, the CDC has given state health departments hundreds of millions of dollars through categorical grant programs to promote mass use of federally recommended vaccines. At the same time, if state health officials do not show federal health officials proof they have attained a certain vaccination rate in their state, federal grants to state health departments can be withheld.

In 1993, the Comprehensive Childhood Immunization Act of 1993 was passed giving the Department of Health and Human Services (DHHS) the authority to award more than $400 million to states to set up state vaccine registries to tag and track children and enforce mandatory vaccination with federally recommended vaccines, including hepatitis B vaccine. The Performance Grant Program rewards a state with either $50, $75 or $100 per child who is fully vaccinated with all federally recommended vaccines, including hepatitis B vaccine and, in 1995, DHHS Secretary Donna Shalala gave the states the power to approve a newborn's social security number in order to set up vaccine tracking registries in more than half the states. The CDC plan is to hook up the state vaccine tracking registries in order to create a de facto centralized electronic database containing every child's medical records.

In 1986, the FDA gave Merck & Co. a license to market the first recombinant DNA hepatitis B vaccine, which replaced the old hepatitis B vaccines made from blood taken from human chronic hepatitis B virus carriers. In awarding Merck & Co. and, later, SmithKline Beecham Pharmaceuticals, licenses to market their genetically engineered hepatitis B vaccines in the U.S., the FDA allowed both drug companies to use "safety" studies which only included a few thousand children monitored for only four or five days after vaccination to check for reactions. As "proof" their hepatitis B vaccine is safe to be used in children, Merck & Co. stated in their 1993 product insert that "In a group of studies, 1636 doses of RECOMBIVAX HB were administered to 653 healthy infants and children (up to 10 years of age) who were monitored for 5 days after each dose."

Merck & Co. found that injection site and systemic complaints, such as fatigue and weakness, fever, headache and arthralgia (joint pain), were reported following up to 17 percent of all hepatitis B injections. Because the FDA did not require drug companies to provide scientific evidence that hepatitis B vaccine does not compromise the immune and neurological systems of children and adults over weeks, months or years post-vaccination, Merck & Co. warns in the 1996 product insert that "As with any vaccine, there is the possibility that broad use of the vaccine could reveal adverse reactions not observed in clinical trials" and SmithKline Beecham (1993) has a similar warning that "it is possible that expanded commercial use of the vaccine could reveal rare adverse reactions.

Another warning in the Merck 1996 product insert is "it is also not known whether the vaccine can cause fetal harm when administered to a pregnant woman or can affect reproduction capacity" and "it is not known whether the vaccine is excreted in human milk. Because many drugs are secreted in human milk, caution should be exercised when the vaccine is administered to a nursing woman."

And, although doctors routinely inject hepatitis B vaccine into children along with many other vaccines such as DPT, HIB, MMR and chickenpox vaccine, Merck & Co. state in the 1996 product insert: "Specific data are not yet available for the simultaneous administration of RECOMBIVAX HB with other vaccines."

All vaccines stimulate only an artificial, temporary immunity, and the length of immunity conferred by the hepatitis B vaccine and the future need for more "booster" doses later in life is still not clear. Merck & Co state in their 1996 hepatitis B vaccine product insert that "the duration of the protective effect of RECOMBIVAX HB in healthy vaccinees is unknown at present and the need for booster doses is not yet defined."

In the *CDC Prevention Guidelines: A Guide to Action* (1997), the CDC states "The duration of protection [of hepatitis B vaccine] and need for booster doses are not yet fully defined. Between 30% and 50% of persons who develop adequate antibody after three doses of vaccine will lose detectable antibody within 7 years but protection against viremic infection and clinical disease appears to persist." If immunity only lasts 7 years, babies vaccinated with hepatitis B vaccine may be candidates for more shots at age seven.

IOM Report Reveals Lack of Adequate Scientific Studies –

In *Adverse Events Associated with Childhood Vaccines* published in 1994 by the Institute of Medicine, National Academy of Sciences, observations about the limitations of hepatitis B vaccine studies included the statements that "it is important to note that individual trials usually involved a few hundred subjects for study...when larger vaccination programs were monitored, observations of adverse events were necessarily less detailed and less accurately reported" and "the studies were not designed to assess serious, rare adverse events; the total number of recipients is too small and the follow-up generally too short to detect rare or delayed serious adverse reactions."

The IOM report also noted that no controlled observational studies or controlled clinical trials have ever been held to evaluate repeated reports that hepatitis B vaccine can cause Guillain-Barré syndrome; arthritis; transverse myelitis, optic neuritis, multiple sclerosis and other central demyelinating diseases of the nervous system (degeneration of the myelin sheath of the brain that helps transmit nerve impulses); or sudden infant death syndrome (SIDS).

A major conclusion of the Institute of Medicine report was that almost no basic science research has been undertaken to define at the cellular and molecular level the biological mechanism of vaccine-induced injury and death. The report concluded that "The lack of adequate data regarding many of the adverse events under study was of major concern to the committee...the committee encountered many gaps and limitations in knowledge bearing directly or indirectly on the safety of vaccines. These include inadequate understanding of the biologic mechanisms underlying adverse events following natural infection or immunization, insufficient or inconsistent information from case reports and case series...and inadequate size or length of follow-up of many population-based epidemiologic studies...."

During the past decade, there have been many reports in the medical literature that hepatitis B vaccination is causing chronic immune and neurological disease in children and adults.

"CONCLUSIONS: Evidence from this study suggests that hepatitis B vaccine is positively associated with adverse health outcomes in the general population of US children."
https://www.ncbi.nlm.nih.gov/pubmed/11164115

The long and the short of it is – every single mother is screened for hepatitis B during pregnancy – so we know which children are at risk and which aren't. Hepatitis B is transmitted through unprotected sex or IV drug use – which hopefully no child on earth is at risk for.

So to give a hepatitis B vaccine on the first day of birth – is nothing short of insanity. Nearly no child is at risk – we know the very few that are ahead of time by screening mothers. There are under 500 cases per year in children – out of 300 million people in the United States.

Also the hepatitis B vaccine does not give permanent immunity – it wanes over time. So injecting your child now will neither guarantee they will be immune now – or later.

The argument is also made that combining the hepatitis B vaccine with the vitamin K shot is an awful idea. Since the vitamin K shot contains Polysorbate 80 – a chemical which is used in animal experiments to open the blood-brain barrier – combining that with a vaccine so high in aluminum could have very dire consequences on a baby's brain. The thing is – there are no true vaccinated vs. unvaccinated studies – so no one can be sure of the possible damage done.

Essentially – people argue that the CDC doctored data by including children that were as young as 6 months of age to skew the data – since autism diagnosis doesn't happen usually until 18 – 24 months.

Hepatitis B has also been linked to diabetes, arthritis, and lupus.

Measles

Before vaccination, the CDC reported 450-500 annual U.S. deaths from measles out of 500,000 – a 0.1% mortality rate.

However, they estimated 3-5 million annual cases were the actual numbers – why? Because they know that beyond the 500,000 documented cases an additional 2.5-4.5 million people got measles and did not seek or need medical attention – since measles is a mild disease that very rarely is accompanied by the need for medical attention. 500 deaths out of 3-5 million cases is a mortality rate of 0.00016%-0.0001%.

The following graph shows the mortality rate of measles falling to nearly zero almost 20 years before the vaccine was introduced.

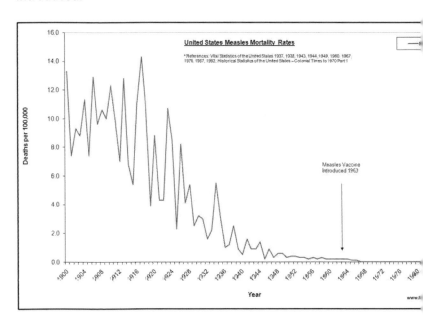

Using the MedAlerts search engine, which facilitates an online search of the federal Vaccine Adverse Events Reporting System (VAERS) database, as of March 3rd, 2016 there have been 7692

serious adverse events Vaccine Adverse Events Reporting System (VAERS) in connection with measles vaccine since 1990, with over half of those occurring in children three years old and under. Of these events 397 were deaths with over half of the deaths occurring in children under three years of age. Remember as well, since VAERS is a passive reporting system – only between 1% and 10% of adverse events actually get reported. Adverse events following MMR vaccination reported to VAERS include:

- Atypical measles (meaning you can get measles from the vaccine)
- lupus (autoimmune connective tissue disorder);
- Guillain-Barré Syndrome (inflammation of the nerves);
- Encephalitis;
- aseptic meningitis (inflammation of the lining of the brain);
- deafness;
- cardiomyopathy (weakening of the heart muscle);
- hypotonic-hyporesponsive episodes (collapse/shock);
- convulsions;
- subacute sclerosing panencephalitis (SSPE);
- ataxia (loss of ability to coordinate muscle movements);
- parathesia (numbness, burning, prickling, itching, tingling skins sensation indicating nerve irritation)
- Transverse Myelitis
- Acute disseminated encephalomyelitis (ADEM)
- Chronic ear infections

Merck also gives the following warnings in their product insert about vaccine strain measles virus infection and shedding:

- " *Measles inclusion body encephalitis (MIBE), pneumonitis and death as a direct consequence of disseminated measles vaccine virus infection have been reported in immunocompromised individuals inadvertently vaccinated with measles-containing* vaccine;" although Merck also states that *"Children and young adults who are known to be infected with human immunodeficiency viruses and are not immunosuppressed may be vaccinated"* and that *"The ACIP has stated that "patients with leukemia in remission who have not received chemotherapy for at least 3 months may receive live virus vaccines. Short-term (<2 weeks), low- to moderate-dose systemic corticosteroid therapy, topical steroid therapy (e.g. nasal, skin), long-term alternate-day 6 treatment with low to moderate doses of short-acting systemic steroid, and intra-articular, bursal, or tendon injection of corticosteroids are not immunosuppressive in their usual doses and do not contraindicate the administration of measles, mumps, or rubella vaccine."*

- *Excretion of small amounts of the live attenuated rubella virus from the nose or throat has occurred in the majority of susceptible individuals 7 to 28 days after vaccination. There is no confirmed evidence to indicate that such virus is transmitted to susceptible persons who are in contact with the vaccinated individuals. Consequently, transmission through close personal contact, while accepted as a theoretical possibility, is not regarded as a significant risk. However, transmission of the rubella vaccine virus to infants via breast milk has been documented."*

- *"There are no reports of transmission of live attenuated measles or mumps viruses from vaccines to susceptible contacts."*

- *"It is not known whether measles or mumps vaccine virus is secreted in human milk. Recent studies have shown that lactating postpartum women immunized with live attenuated rubella vaccine may secrete the virus in breast milk and transmit it to breast-fed infants. In the infants with serological evidence of rubella infection, none exhibited severe disease; however, one exhibited mild clinical illness typical of acquired rubella."*

"There have been reports of subacute sclerosing panencephalitis (SSPE) in children who did not have a history of infection with wild-type measles but did receive measles vaccine. Some of these cases may have resulted from unrecognized measles in the first year of life or possibly from the measles vaccination."

Merck has been the subject of a lawsuit since 2012 in which 2 employees of Merck claim they were told to spike data samples or flat-out lie about the results.

Merck attempted to get the FDA to settle this out of court – but the judge denied the attempt because they were defrauding the U.S. government (because they are the sole owners of the MMR vaccine patent and the U.S. government is a large client). It is still ongoing as of the writing of this book.

You can very easily find updates on the web if you look for them – as there are quite a few.

Here are another few examples of Merck's "honesty".

Big Pharma bombshell: Judge finds Merck lied in patent trial, overturns $200-million verdict:
http://www.latimes.com/business/hiltzik/la-fi-hiltzik-merck-gilead-20160608-snap-story.html

Merck told to pay $950 Million over marketing and sales of Vioxx
http://www.nytimes.com/2011/11/23/business/merck-agrees-to-pay-950-million-in-vioxx-case.html

Merck made a "hit list" of doctors who criticized Vioxx, according to testimony in a Vioxx class action case in Australia. The list, emailed between Merck employees, contained doctors' names with the labels "neutralise," "neutralised" or "discredit" next to them.
http://www.cbsnews.com/news/merck-created-hit-list-to-destroy-neutralize-or-discredit-dissenting-doctors/
(The Wakefield story gets more interesting now, doesn't it?)

Merck's Zostavax Drug Hit With Lawsuits for not disclosing side effects

http://www.investopedia.com/news/mercks-zostavax-drug-hit-lawsuits-mrk-gsk/

Also measles outbreaks have occurred in highly or completely vaccinated individuals and populations – which may be due in part to the lawsuit that is mentioned above.

https://www.ncbi.nlm.nih.gov/pubmed/8053748

"We found 18 reports of measles outbreaks in very highly immunized school populations where 71% to 99.8% of students were immunized against measles. Despite these high rates of immunization, 30% to 100% (mean, 77%) of all measles cases in these outbreaks occurred in previously immunized students. In our hypothetical school model, after more than 95% of schoolchildren are immunized against measles, the majority of measles cases occur in appropriately immunized children.

"The apparent paradox is that as measles immunization rates rise to high levels in a population, measles becomes a disease of immunized persons. Because of the failure rate of the vaccine and the unique transmissibility of the measles virus, the currently available measles vaccine, used in a single-dose strategy, is unlikely to completely eliminate measles. The long-term success of a two-dose strategy to eliminate measles remains to be determined."

The CDC now currently recommends 3 doses of the MMR vaccine instead of the 1 or 2 that were used before due to the outbreaks in highly vaccinated populations and individuals.

There is also the William Thompson subject and Andrew Wakefield as well. However since there is so much argument on each side I encourage you to research these on your own.

The William Thompson topic is a CDC researcher who claimed that he was ordered to destroy large quantities of data showing the MMR vaccine was linked to a spike in autism – however proponents claim that his work was not sound.

The CDC somehow blocked him from testifying at a congressional hearing so he could never give his story in a court. He is still employed at the CDC.

Andrew Wakefield was the doctor who published his paper on the MMR vaccine causing intestinal issues seen in many autistic kids – something he never set out to prove. Out of 10 doctors who signed off on the paper – he was the only one that lost his license. He also was the only one that spoke up. However – you should dig further and see what your opinion is on the matter. The "behind the scenes" in the movie "Vaxxed" is a wonderful resource to hear him tell his personal story.

Also – there are hundreds of clinical trials on how measles can be cured with vitamin C and vitamin A. Even the CDC says on their page that vitamin A is an effective treatment for measles. You can decide how worried about a disease that can be cured by carrots and lemons you should be – hit up www.scholar.google.com and do a search for "measles and vitamin" – you'll have more than enough thousand studies to keep you busy for a while.

For these next two there isn't a whole lot to collect as far as information goes – so this book will not be a good resource as far as your decision goes on if you want to vaccinate for them or not.

I will however give you the statistics on how deadly they actually are (or not).

That is always a great starting point.

Mumps

Before vaccination started, the CDC reported 186,000 annual mumps cases. "The actual number of cases was likely much higher due to underreporting." Mumps was added to the vaccination schedule in 1967. From 1960 to 1966 the average annual deaths according to the CDC from mumps was 44. That's a mortality rate of 0.02%

However that number is based on 186,000 reported cases and as mumps is fairly mild - and the CDC even admits the 186,000 annual cases is likely to be much higher – lowering the true mortality rate to well below 0.02%.

Rubella

Rubella vaccination began in 1969. According to the CDC, "During the last major rubella epidemic in the United States from 1964 to 1965, an estimated 12.5 million people got rubella."

The CDC statistics report that in 1964 and 1965 there were a total of 69 deaths from rubella. 69 deaths out of 12.5 million cases is a mortality rate of 0.0005%.

Polio

This one is an especially interesting story – and extremely complex so I'll do my very best to simplify it as best as possible without getting too far off track.

Polio – also called Poliomyolitis – is an enterovirus that can cause paralysis in a very small number of cases. 95% of people who contract polio clear the infection without even knowing they have it. About 1-5% develop slightly more serious symptoms like a flu-like illness or a stiff neck. About 0.1%-2% of cases develop the more serious version where paralysis or death can occur.

Here becomes the problem – we have absolutely no idea what the actual cases of polio were before – or after the vaccination.

Let's first examine the actual data on polio quick:

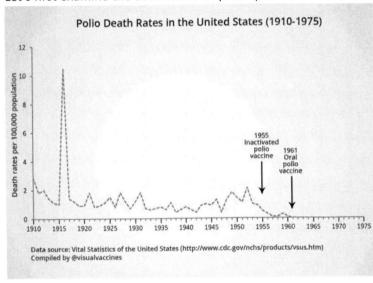

Polio Death Rates in the United States (1910-1975)

Data source: Vital Statistics of the United States (http://www.cdc.gov/nchs/products/vsus.htm)
Compiled by @visualvaccines

128

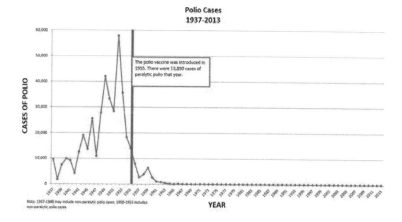

Polio Cases
1937-2013

From the data we can see the number of polio cases both rose and fell with our without the vaccine, as did the death rates. But here's where it gets interesting.

Prior to vaccination – anyone who would come into a doctor's office complaining of the stiff neck or paralysis was declared to have polio without any form of testing – despite there possibly being something else that caused the symptoms (different enteroviruses can cause this, as can systemic poisoning from different chemicals – such as DDT, but more on this in a bit).

In order to be diagnosed with polio you had to complain of symptoms of paralysis or other symptoms for 24-48 hours and get 2 examinations within that time period.

Now here's where it gets interesting.

In the exact same year that the polio vaccine was introduced, the diagnostic criteria was changed in multiple ways.

First – your symptoms had to last for 60-90 days instead of 1-2 days.

Additionally, to be declared to have polio – you actually had to get tested for polio.

So here's the problem. **I'm going to paint an EXTREMELY outrageous picture** – but only to illustrate a point.

Let's say that I wanted to release a vaccine for the flu. Right now – you only have to have symptoms for a few days to get diagnosed with the flu.

So let's say I urinate in a glass – and claim my urine will protect you from the flu if you inject yourself with it.

Sounds absurd, right?

Well now let's take – and change – the diagnostic criteria for the flu at the same time that I release said piss-filled vaccine.

Now instead of a few days of symptoms – you have to have 60-90 days of flu-like symptoms.

Also – every person who wants to claim they have the flu has to be tested to confirm they have some strain of the flu virus causing the symptoms, where they did not have to before.

This certainly would make it appear like injecting my urine dropped the cases of the flu by an exceptional number, wouldn't it?

Well – the exact same scenario happened with the release of the polio vaccine.

In the same year that the vaccine was released – the diagnostic criteria changed drastically – and they started testing for the polio virus to ensure people actually had the polio virus when they were diagnosed with it.

So – wouldn't that skew the data completely?

I'm not saying my urine will cure the flu.

I only painted an exceptionally outrageous picture to prove a point.

It is absolutely in no way shape or form possible to attribute any drop in the number or severity of polio cases in America from strictly the polio vaccine when so many other factors are at play.

"When the tide is receding from the beach, it is easy to have the illusion that one can empty the ocean by removing the water with a pail."
~Rene Dubos in "Mirage of Health"

Dr. Suzanne Humphries published 2 wonderful books called "Vaccines – Dissolving Illusions" and "Smoke, Mirrors, and the disappearance of Polio" – I highly suggest people look those up.

Here's what further complicates the problem:

DDT.

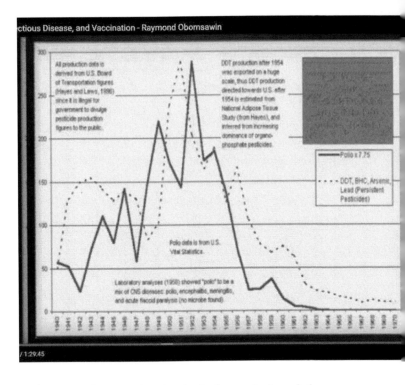

Symptoms of DDT poisoning include respiratory failure, paralysis, joint stiffness, fever, and death – essentially the exact same symptoms "polio" has.

Remember, this was a time when we used to spray kids in the face with DDT, the kids would chase the trucks down the road while they sprayed it, and it was added to the wallpapers in kids' rooms to help keep bugs down. (If you think we've wised up any since – you'd be wrong. Just look at how much RoundUp we spray today. We've learned nothing apparently.)

DDT was banned/phased out at nearly the exact same time the polio vaccine was released as well.

So adding that to the mixture certainly complicates things, doesn't it? So how could anyone say – after learning about all of these variables – that the polio vaccine alone eradicated polio?

One could argue that the polio vaccine did absolutely nothing – and be able to make a case for that. I'm not saying that – I'm just saying if that's what someone said you couldn't say they were wrong.

In fact – they could certainly raise a very strong argument.

We however haven't even touched on how we don't use the same polio vaccine today, the cutter incident, and a lot more.

Here's where it gets REALLY fun.

A few years back (before it was deleted due to public backlash) the CDC admitted that roughly 90 million Americans were given a polio vaccine that contained a retrovirus called SV-40 that causes cancer. You can still find the links that have been archived if you look for them fairly easily, as well as the research to show that SV-40 is indeed a harmful retrovirus. Remember when I had you ask the doctor if they could provide test results proving that the vaccine you or your child would get was free of retroviruses?

This is why you ask that question – and we haven't even gotten into Garth Nicolson yet (probably won't either – most people don't have the stomach for it). There is conflicting views over whether SV-40 causes cancer or not – so I suggest you research for yourself and decide what you think. I would, however, encourage you not to fully trust what the CDC says on SV-40 – since they have a habit of deleting things that don't look good for them.

I also encourage readers to at least read this information: http://www.naturalnews.com/033584_Dr_Maurice_Hilleman_S V40.html Yes – I know Natural News is "Fake News". I'm not asking you to believe anything the guy says – I'm only asking you to hear what Dr. Maurice Hilleman (a vaccine scientist at Merck) has to say in an interview about vaccines being contaminated with over 40 different retroviruses.

This is why I encourage readers to get lab results showing that their vaccines are free from retrovirus contamination. This isn't to scare you – it's simply a reality that is all too often overlooked.

Remember, too – the CDC said the Zikapocalypse was coming, swine flu would kill huge quantities of people, avian flu, you get the idea. It is always a good idea to use multiple sources – not just one that is responsible for both vaccine safety and vaccine promotion at the same time – and that owns multiple patents on vaccines. Just saying.

Now that you've got a partial history on polio – you hopefully can make an educated decision when it comes time to have anyone in your family get the vaccine or not.

I'm not saying to not get it – I'm just making sure you're informed before you do (with more than just a sticker and a lollipop) that the history on the disease is...a little dirty.

Finally I include a link to this breakdown so you can read it all for yourself because it breaks it all down beautifully on how the use of pesticides was a major cause to what the United States called "Polio" – I HIGHLY suggest you read this breakdown:

https://www.westonaprice.org/health-topics/environmental-

Finally – just to really let this information hit home – talk a look at this advertisement. It will probably speak for itself.

We also now spray all our food with poison made from this same company under the claim that it's "safe" – we haven't learned much have we.

Varicella (chickenpox)

Before vaccination the CDC reported almost 4 million cases annually with around 100 deaths. That's a 0.0025 chance of death from the chickenpox.

For comparison the CDC also reports about 450 people a year die from falling out of bed. So according to the CDC before they vaccinated for chickenpox you were 4 times more likely to die from falling out of bed than from this disease.

To quote a brilliant nutritionist and epigeneticist, Sterling Hill:

"Of course we don't want things like AIDS or Ebola but I will give you an example of a virus that is crucial for us and can literally take 20-30 years off of your life if you do not have this virus in you.
We know all children with severe autism have active HSV.
We know all children with autism have leaky gut and hyperoxaluria.
Hold on and you will see what I am getting at.
When we get chickenpox as a child, it is mother nature doing an initial oxalate purge. The more oxalate in the body the more pustules you will see.
Now the chickenpox virus goes and lays on the base of the skull as shingles.
This virus is there to save you later on in life.
When the body can no longer excrete oxalate from the kidneys and under times of stress when the body is dumping b6 and zinc it will make endogenous oxalate.
Well if you cannot excrete from the kidneys the shingles virus will come out of dormancy and remove oxalate via a nerve path on the skin.
Those blisters like chickenpox pustules are oxalate content coming out of your body.
If your body is unable to remove oxalate you will eventually die.
Oxalate and sulfate share a transporter called SLC26A1 and when the oxalate start hogging up the transporters, we stop sulfating so the shingles virus is trying to get you to be able to

sulfate again by removing excess oxalate.

By preventing the chickenpox virus I fear that many will have shorter life spans."

Long story short – just like the measles virus is being used to train the immune system to fight cancer – the chickenpox virus can also be used to help train the body to fight other diseases. It can be akin to thinking of these benign diseases as sparring partners for the immune system. Overall – this sparring partner is less deadly than your risk of falling out of bed – and can come with some benefits as well.

As this researcher states:

"The universal varicella (chickenpox) vaccination program now requires a booster vaccine for children and a HZ vaccine to boost protection in adults.

However, these are less effective than the natural immunity that existed in communities prior to licensure of the varicella vaccine.

Hence, rather than eliminating varicella in children as promised, routine vaccination against varicella has proven extremely costly and has created continual cycles of treatment and disease."

https://www.ncbi.nlm.nih.gov/pmc/articles/PMC3759842/#sec 0150title

Also just to point out – the vaccine itself does carry risks outside of not offering permanent protection:

- As of September 1, 2015, there had been 122 claims filed in the federal Vaccine Injury Compensation Program (VICP) for injuries and deaths following chickenpox or varicella vaccination, including 8 deaths and 114 serious injuries.
- Using the MedAlerts search engine, as of September 30, 2015 there had been 3,358 serious adverse events reported to the Vaccine Adverse Events Reporting System (VAERS) in connection with chickenpox and varicella-containing vaccines since 1990. Over half of those serious chickenpox vaccine-related adverse events occurring in children six years old and under. Of these chickenpox-vaccine related adverse event reports to VAERS, 161 were deaths, with over 60% of the deaths occurring in children under six years of age.

Also recall where we brought up the problem earlier – only between 1% - 10% of vaccine injuries or adverse events ever get reported – due to VAERS being a passive reporting system – so these numbers could be much higher. I'm not saying I know how much higher – I'm just saying there is no active tracking so we can be sure.

Chickenpox Vaccine

- There are two live virus vaccines for chickenpox licensed in the U.S.: Varivax and ProQuad (MMRV) manufactured by Merck;
- The CDC recommends children get a chickenpox shot at 12 months old and a booster dose between 4 and 6 years old;
- Reported complications from chickenpox vaccine include shock, seizures, brain inflammation (encephalitis), thrombocytopenia (blood disorder), Guillain-Barré Syndrome, death and infection with vaccine strain chickenpox or transmission of vaccine strain chickenpox to others;

- Chickenpox vaccine effectiveness is reported to be 44 percent for any form of the disease and 86 percent for moderate to severe disease;
- Mass use of chickenpox vaccine by children in the U.S. has removed natural boosting of immunity in the population, which was protective against shingles, and now adults are experiencing a shingles epidemic

Many doctors argue that getting chickenpox (like measles) is beneficial later on in life – example:

History of chickenpox in glioma risk: a report from the glioma international case–control study (GICC)

In one of the largest studies to date, an international consortium led by researchers in the Dan L Duncan Comprehensive Cancer Center at Baylor College of Medicine reported an inverse relationship between a history of chickenpox and glioma, a type of brain cancer, meaning that children who have had the chickenpox may be less likely to develop brain cancer.

http://onlinelibrary.wiley.com/doi/10.1002/cam4.682/abstract; jsessionid=63C3E90E9A0DE827F5CFD7259139FDAA.f02t01

Meningococcal

According to the CDC....

"Meningococcal vaccines help protect against the bacteria that cause meningococcal disease. These infections don't happen very often, but can be very dangerous when they do.

Meningococcal disease refers to any illness that is caused by *Neisseria meningitidis* bacteria.

"The two most severe and common illnesses caused by these bacteria include infections of the fluid and lining around the brain and spinal cord (meningitis(https://www.cdc.gov/meningitis/index.html)) and bloodstream infections (bacteremia or septicemia).

"Even if they get treatment, about 10 to 15 out of 100 people with meningococcal disease will die from it. Meningococcal disease can spread from person to person. The bacteria that cause this infection can spread when people have close or lengthy contact with someone's saliva, like through kissing or coughing, especially if they are living in the same place.

"Teens and young adults are at increased risk for meningococcal disease. Meningococcal disease can become very serious, very quickly."

According to the CDC website, during 2005-2011 an estimated 800-1,200 cases of meningococcal disease occurred annually in the United States, representing an incidence of 0.3 cases per 100,000 population. With a 2010 U.S. population of 308,000,000 that means infection occurs in 0.00038% of the population. The case-fatality ratio for meningococcal disease is between 10-14% (CDC, 2005). Each year in the U.S. it is estimated that between 80-120 people die from meningococcal infection. This makes your chances of dying from meningococcal infection one in several million.

Meningitis is also a fatal side effect of the meningococcal vaccine. Previous vaccination with viral vaccines (think hepatitis B at birth) damages the terminal complement portion of the immune system, leaving the patient more vulnerable to meningococcal infection. When are our children most vulnerable to meningococcal infection? Infancy, junior high, and their freshman year of college.

Why? Possibly because that's when they are receiving multiple vaccines for viral infections, and multiple vaccines that are contaminated with unknown numbers of viruses.

According to The Center for Disease Control (CDC), about 1 in 10 folks have the Neisseria meningitidis bacteria in the back of their throat, but have no symptoms of the disease. These folks are considered carriers.

The Neisseria meningitides bacteria is broken down into five strains called A, B, C, W, and Y. Parents who dutifully follow the CDC vaccination rulebook inject their 11 – 12-year-old child with a vaccine that is supposed to protect them from the A, C, W and Y strains.

However, it was the B strain that caused meningitis outbreaks at the University of California, San Diego (UCSD) in March of 2013. The same B strain also caused the outbreak at Princeton in November of 2013. During both of these events, there was no FDA approved vaccine for the B strain. But what do you know, just three months before the UCSD outbreak, the European Union (EU) approved Bexsero, the world's first vaccination for the B strain of Neisseria meningitides, created by pharmaceutical giant Novartis.

Follow the timeline: Bexsero is approved in the EU in January 2013; College outbreaks occur in March and November, 2013; And by December 2013, the universities demanded that this new Bexsero vaccine be made available to their students, even though it wasn't licensed for use in the U.S. Therefore, the students got their shots.

Now if we fast forward to January, 2015, the FDA not only **approved Bexsero**, but recommended it for most individuals between the age of 10 – 25. Even some U.S. physicians believed this approval was a little **too fast and maybe not so safe.** Health Impact News has the details:

"Dr. Mark Sawyer, an infectious disease specialist at Rady Children's Hospital in San Diego, told reporters... 'Newer vaccines on the market lack comprehensive evidence on safety and effectiveness, compared with vaccines that have been administered to tens of millions of people over decades.'

[Dr. Sawyer also told reporters] that he did not vaccinate his own daughter because he did not feel that she was at an increased risk."

But wait, there's more. Pfizer, another mega pharmaceutical company, was also busy creating and marketing Trumenba, an addtional vaccine for this B strain meningitis.

It was reviewed, **according** to the FDA, "and approved under the FDA's Breakthrough Therapy designation and Priority Review programs." This fast track approval for Trumenba took place in October 2014, *prior* to Bexsero FDA approval.

But Trumenba expanded their market share and said it would be good for ages 10 – 25. And when Bexsero was approved in January 2015, Novartis added that demographic of 10 – 25 years of age as well.

So now, two vaccines exist for this B strain of meningitis. In the U.S., both were allowed to be used before they were licensed. Now, in the UK, these same vaccines are now being marketed for infants. But what about the ingredients? Health Impact News has the specifics:

"... The Bexsero vaccination contains 1.5 mg of **aluminium**, which is a massive 1475 mcg more than the FDA's "safe" recommended amount. Another interesting fact is that according to the CDC one of the ingredients [that both these vaccines contain]... is *E.coli* and this was not listed by the manufacturer."

Appendix B

Vaccine	Contains	Source: Manufacturer's P.I. Dated
Influenza (FluMist) Quadrivalent	ethylene diamine tetraacetic acid (EDTA), monosodium glutamate, hydrolyzed porcine gelatin, arginine, sucrose, dibasic potassium phosphate, monobasic potassium phosphate, gentamicin sulfate, egg protein	July 2013
Japanese Encephalitis (Ixiaro)	aluminum hydroxide, Vero cells, protamine sulfate, formaldehyde, bovine serum albumin, sodium metabisulphite, sucrose	May 2013
Meningococcal (MCV4-Menactra)	formaldehyde, phosphate buffers, Mueller Hinton agar, Watson Scherp media, Modified Mueller and Miller medium, detergent, alcohol, ammonium sulfate	April 2013
Meningococcal (MCV4-Menveo)	formaldehyde, amino acids, yeast extract, Franz complete medium, CY medium	August 2013
Meningococcal (MPSV4-Menomune)	thimerosal (multi-dose vial only), lactose, Mueller Hinton casein agar, Watson Scherp media, detergent, alcohol	April 2013
Meningococcal (MenB – Bexsero)	aluminum hydroxide, *E. coli*, histidine, sucrose, deoxycholate, kanomycin	2015
Meningococcal (MenB – Trumenba)	polysorbate 80, histodine, *E. coli*, fermentation growth media	October 2015
MMR (MMR-II)	Medium 199 (vitamins, amino acids, fetal bovine serum, sucrose, glutamate), Minimum Essential Medium, phosphate, recombinant human albumin, neomycin, sorbitol, hydrolyzed gelatin, chick embryo cell culture, WI-38 human diploid lung fibroblasts	June 2014

Let's break it down quickly:

- At any given time, about 20 to 40 percent of Americans are asymptomatically colonizing meningococcal organisms in their nasal passages and throats, which throughout life boosts innate immunity to invasive meningococcal infection. Mothers, who have innate immunity, transfer maternal antibodies to their newborns to protect them in the first few months of life until babies can make their own antibodies. By the time American children enter adolescence, the vast majority have asymptomatically developed immunity that protects them;
- A small minority of individuals who have genetic and other unknown biological factors which prevent them from naturally

developing protective circulating antibodies are up to 7,000 times more likely to get severe invasive meningococcal disease at some point in their lives;

- In addition to genetic factors, high-risk factors for developing invasive meningococcal infection include smoking or living in a home where people smoke; a recent respiratory infection; crowded living conditions, such as in military and prisons settings; alcohol use; and an underlying chronic illness, especially immune deficiencies such as lupus or HIV/AIDS;
- Only one in a couple million people will die of meningococcal disease yearly.

Meningococcal Vaccine

- There are six meningococcal vaccines licensed and marketed in the U.S.: Bexsero, MenHibrix, Menactra, Menomune, Menveo and Trumenba;
- In 2000, the CDC recommended that all college freshmen get a dose of meningococcal vaccine containing four strains (A, C, W-35, Y) and, in 2005, that policy was expanded to include all 11-year-olds.
- In 2016 2 vaccines containing strain B, which is the strain associated with more than 50 percent of meningococcal cases and deaths, especially in children under five years old, was approved by the FDA;
- The meningococcal vaccine has been found to be about 58 percent effective within two to five years after adolescents have gotten the shot and, in 2011, CDC recommended that all 16-year-olds get a booster dose of meningococcal vaccine;
- The manufacturer product inserts for meningococcal vaccine list adverse events reported during clinical trials or post licensure, including irritability, abnormal crying, fever, drowsiness, fatigue, injection site pain and swelling, sudden loss of consciousness (syncope), diarrhea, headache, joint pain, Guillain-Barré Syndrome, brain inflammation, convulsions, facial palsy, and death.

- As of September 1, 2015, there had been 47 claims filed in the federal Vaccine Injury Compensation Program (VICP) for injuries and deaths following meningococcal vaccination, including 2 deaths and 45 serious injuries.

- Using the MedAlerts search engine, as of September 30, 2015, the federal Vaccine Adverse Events Reporting System (VAERS), which includes only a small fraction of the health problems that occur after vaccination in the U.S., had recorded more than 1,846 serious health problems, hospitalizations and injuries following meningococcal shots, including 99 deaths with about 34% of the deaths occurring in children under age six.

2000 CDC report on the meningococcal disease in the U.S.

https://www.cdc.gov/mmwr/preview/mmwrhtml/rr4907a2.htm

Following information is a summary from the 2000 CDC report:

1- 1990-1991 - A questionnaire designed to evaluate risk factors for meningococcal disease among college students was sent to 1900 universities, resulting in a 38% response rate.

Forty-three cases of meningococcal disease were reported during the 2 years from colleges with a total enrollment of 4,393,744 students, for a low overall incidence of 1.0 per 100,000 population per year.

However, cases of meningococcal disease occurred 9-23 times more frequently in students residing in dormitories than in those residing in other types of accommodations. The low response rate and the inability of the study to control for other factors make these results difficult to interpret.

2- 1998-1999 – U.S. started to keep track of the disease in college students. In this time period 90 cases were reported to the CDC. These cases represent approximately 3% of the total cases that occur each year in the United States. Eighty-seven cases occurred in undergraduate students, and 40% occurred among the 2.27 million freshmen students. Eight students died. [This data suggests that the overall rate of disease among undergraduate college students is lower than the rate among persons aged 18-23 years who are not enrolled in college. Even though the rates were higher in freshmen students (4.6/100,000) living in dormitories, it was still lower than the threshold of 10/100,000 recommended for initiating meningococcal vaccination campaigns.]

Also – possibly due to the high aluminum content in certain vaccines (like the HPV vaccine):

"Analysis Shows Greater Risk of GBS Reports When HPV Vaccine Is Given with Meningococcal and Other Vaccines"

http://www.nvic.org/vaccines-and-diseases/HPV/hpvaug152007.aspx

Robert F Kennedy did the math on the meningococcal vaccine and I quote:

"According to their package inserts, Menactra and Menveo produce 'serious adverse events' in 1 percent of recipients. Menomune, with its hefty mercury load, sickens 1.3 percent of those receiving it.

"According to the CDC Pink Book, 0.3 percent of those with 'serious adverse events' from meningitis vaccines will die. So here is the math calculation that thoughtful student governments in Colorado must consider:

"If you inoculate Colorado's 400,000 college students with the older vaccines, you can expect 4,000 serious adverse events and 12 dead. We do not yet know the effects of widespread vaccination of the hastily-expedited B vaccines, but according to their package inserts, about 2 percent of students who receive the B vaccine will be sickened or hospitalized with a serious adverse event.

"This could translate into an additional 8,000 sick students and 24 deaths, for a total of 12,000 sick and 36 dead in the attempt to possibly avert three meningitis cases.

"The budgetary issues are significant. Administering Bexsero will cost an estimated $320 per student according to the CDC vaccine price list. For Colorado's 400,000 students, the cost for the B vaccine alone would be $128 million annually.

"Vaccine makers stand to make over a billion dollars annually if they can persuade the ACIP to add their meningitis vaccines to the national schedule. While there is huge corporate incentive to get these vaccines mandated in the Colorado higher education system, the costs of this mandate, in both dollars and students' lives, are sobering.

"The calculation could make sense only to cold-blooded bean counters at the companies marketing these vaccines and to politicians who have collected those companies' 'contributions.'"

RV (rotavirus) vaccine

(Only recommended in three first world countries.)

"For Rotavirus, a vaccine commercially available now for 11 years, the numbers are laughable: Of 29 other first world countries that GR evaluated, only 2 also mandate Rotavirus. Said differently, 27 of 29 other first world countries besides the

United States DO NOT think Rotavirus is an important enough disease that the children of their country should receive a vaccine for it, even though a vaccine has been available for over a decade."

According to the CDC, "Every year before the vaccine was available more than 400,000 young children had to see a doctor for illness caused by rotavirus, and 20 to 60 died." That's a mortality rate of 0.005% - 0.015%.

Rotavirus is the most common cause of *severe* diarrhea among children worldwide.There are many different strains of rotavirus that can infect humans or animals, including monkeys, cows, and sheep. There are <u>five main strains</u> that cause more than 90 percent of human rotavirus infections in developed countries such as the U.S., but rotavirus strains are more diverse in developing countries. Infants younger than three months old may not develop diarrhea symptoms when they are infected with rotavirus because they have maternal antibodies transferred from their mother to protect them in the first few months of life, including through breastfeeding. By the age of five, most children have had several rotavirus infections and have developed natural antibodies that protect them from symptoms of diarrhea when they are re-infected as they get older.

CDC Admits That Merck's RotaTeq Rotavirus Vaccine is Causing Intussusception (Severe Bowel Obstruction) in Infants.
Excerpt: "A new CDC study shows 272 reports of intussusception (severe bowel obstruction) after the first dose of Merck's rotavirus vaccine RotaTeq. The first rotavirus vaccine (Rotashield) was pulled from the market after similar reports. There are now 202 infant deaths (age < 3years) associated with Rotateq in the FDA Vaccine Adverse Event Reporting System (VAERS)."
https://www.cdc.gov/vaccines/vpd-vac/rotavirus/vac-rotashield-historical.htm

"Infants who receive the rotavirus vaccine, which protects against a severe diarrheal disease, may have a very small risk of developing a serious intestinal disorder called intussusception, a new study finds."

http://www.livescience.com/42544-rotavirus-vaccine-side-effect-intussusception.html

From 1985-1991, pediatric deaths in the U.S. from diarrhea from ALL causes numbered around 300 per year: http://www.ncbi.nlm.nih.gov/pubmed/7563485 ALL causes. That means diarrhea from every single intestinal virus, every food-borne illness, every case of food poisoning, even diarrhea caused by too much Hallowe'en candy. ALL causes.

After the introduction of the rotavirus vaccine, that number nearly doubled.

By these numbers that means:

Since rotavirus vaccines were introduced, pediatric diarrhea deaths have INCREASED.

By 2010, the CDC separated pediatric diarrheal deaths into several different categories:

316 diarrhea and gastrointestinal from infectious origin

29 gastritis, duodenitis, and non-infective enteritis and colitis

51 hernia of abdominal cavity and obstruction without hernia

124 all other and unspecified diseases of digestive system.

Total: 520 pediatric deaths due to intestinal issues that cause diarrhea

http://www.cdc.gov/nchs/data/nvsr/nvsr61/nvsr61_04.pdf

On top of that, rotavirus vaccines, not surprisingly, cause some pretty severe adverse reactions—including diarrhea, vomiting, and a life-threatening condition called intussusception. Reported adverse reactions from the vaccine range from 490 to 819 per year.

So, not only have diarrhea deaths increased since introduction of rotavirus vaccines, but the vaccines are causing hundreds of severe adverse reactions per year.

On May 7, 2010, the FDA announced that RotaTeq vaccine was contaminated with DNA from two porcine circoviruses: PCV1 and PCV2. To date the vaccine manufacturer, Merck, has not given any information regarding if, or when, PCV1 and PCV2 will be removed from this vaccine. Although PCV1 has not been associated with clinical disease in pigs, PCV2 is a lethal pig virus that causes immune suppression and a serious wasting disease in baby pigs that damages lungs, kidneys, the reproductive system, brain and ultimately causes death. The FDA recommended temporary suspension of the use of Rotarix vaccine on March 22nd after DNA from PCV1 was identified in Rotarix, but did not call for suspension of the use of RotaTeq vaccine after PCV2 was found in RotaTeq. On June 1st, NVIC called on Merck to volunartarily withdraw RotaTeq from the market until PCV2, especially, is removed from the vaccine.

RotaTeq vaccine is manufactured by Merck and was licensed by the FDA in 2006.

Description: RotaTeq is a genetically engineered vaccine made of live, attenuated human-bovine hybridized reassortant rotaviruses. Other ingredients include sucrose, sodium citrate, sodium phosphate monobasic monohydrate, sodium hydroxide, polysorbate 80, cell culture media, and trace amounts of fetal bovine serum. It does not contain preservatives.

According to the Merck manufacturer product information package insert, there is:
• *No safety or efficacy data available from clinical trials regarding the administration of RotaTeq to infants who are potentially immunocompromised*
• *No safety or efficacy data available for the administration of RotaTeq to infants with a history of gastrointestinal disorders (e.g., active acute gastrointestinal illness, chronic diarrhea, failure*
to thrive, history of congenital abdominal disorders, abdominal surgery and intussusception).

"Live pentavalent human–bovine reassortant rotavirus vaccine is recommended in the United States for routine immunization of infants. We describe three infants, two with failure to thrive, who had dehydration and diarrhea within 1 month after their first or second rotavirus immunization and subsequently received a diagnosis of severe combined immunodeficiency. Rotavirus was detected, by means of reverse-transcriptase–polymerase-chain-reaction (RT-PCR) assay, in stool specimens obtained from all three infants, and gene-sequence analysis revealed the presence of vaccine rotavirus. These infections raise concerns regarding the safety of rotavirus vaccine in severely immunocompromised patients."
http://www.nejm.org/doi/full/10.1056/NEJMoa0904485

"Conclusions. Intussusception and gastroenteritis were the most commonly reported outcomes; however, a substantial number of reports indicate signs and symptoms consistent with either illness, possibly suggestive of a spectrum of gastrointestinal illness(es) related to RRV-TV."

http://pediatrics.aappublications.org/content/113/4/e353.full

The most interesting part of the RotaTeq vaccine is an individual named Paul Offit.

Paul Offit is the co-developer of the RotaTeq vaccine and is the head of the Philadelphia Children's Hospital, where he does vaccine research. Offit has gone on record stating that an infant's immune system could theoretically handle 10,000 vaccines at once.

He also sat on the board of the CDC that recommends vaccines to the current vaccine schedule, before taking his lucrative position at the Children's Hospital.

After developing his vaccine, Offit sold the patent on it for up $60 million dollars (the total sale price was $180 million – we however do not know how much he made from the vaccine sale – as he will not say). This normally would just be business – and happens all the time. The problem comes in here:

Four months before Offit was appointed to ACIP in October 1998, the committee had voted to give the rotavirus category a "Routine Vaccination" status, in anticipation of an FDA approval of RotaShield (oddly, ACIP made this vote before the FDA approved Wyeth's RotaShield vaccine on October 1, 1998).

Shortly after Offit's term began, there were several additional votes involved in establishing the rotavirus vaccine market and Offit voted yes in every case.

In May of 1999, the CDC published its revised childhood vaccination schedule and rotavirus vaccine was included. This series of favorable votes clearly enhanced the monetary value of Offit's stake in Merck's rotavirus vaccine, which was five years into clinical trials.

Nevertheless, Merck's RotaTeq vaccine was several years behind Wyeth's RotaShield, which stood to be the market leader based on its lead in making its way through clinical trials. But when the widespread administration of RotaShield to infants started producing a high incidence of intussusception reports, including numerous fatalities, ACIP was forced to reverse itself.

On October 22, 1999, ACIP voted to rescind its recommendation of the RotaShield vaccine.

Offit recused himself from this vote, although he participated in the discussion. In the meeting in which ACIP discussed RotaShield, Offit remarked, "I'm not conflicted with Wyeth, but because I consult with Merck on the development of rotavirus vaccine, I would still prefer to abstain because it creates a perception of conflict."

CDC records make it clear that Offit was not silent on RotaShield. By 2001, he was actively advancing a "unique strain" hypothesis, an argument that RotaShield was formulated in a way that did increase intussusception risk whereas other formulations (e.g. Rotateq) would not.

In commercial terms, Offit had a clear stake in the earlier RotaShield decision. As a competitor to Rotateq, RotaShield's withdrawal provided a financial opportunity for Offit's partner, Merck.

Not only did RotaShield's withdrawal give Rotateq an opportunity to gain 100% of the rotavirus vaccine market Offit had voted to create (until April 2008, when GlaxoSmithKline's Rotarix vaccine was approved, Merck held a monopoly on the rotavirus vaccine market), but the absence of competition enabled Merck to charge a premium price for its vaccine, significantly more than Wyeth had charged for RotaShield.

So the long story short is – the guy holding the patent on the vaccine was able to vote whether or not it should be on the infant vaccine schedule – and have a say in influencing whether or not his competitor's vaccine should still be on the market.

Paul Offit regularly gives talks to confront "Vaccine Deniers" (that is – people who don't believe everything they're told about vaccines) – but has refused to do any sort of open discussion with those that question his "science" (including his statement that infants could handle up to 10,000 vaccines at once. Funny enough multiple petitions at the White House have been started asking Paul to take all those vaccines at once. Sadly nothing has come of it). In fact – he was quite fond of four-letter words when the producers of the movie "Vaxxed" tried to ask him to sit down and visit with them on camera about vaccines and his beliefs. Even funnier – he was at a conference at the time teaching people how to confront "Vaccine Deniers".

Since he has refused to do any sort of interviews publicly on camera with people who question his stance – there are multiple people that have done a "virtual debate" where they take pieces of what he has said on camera and discuss his faulty science. One exceptional piece I like can be found at the link below. It should be noted, since Mr. Offit doesn't have a chance to respond – it is slightly unfair to him. However, he has been given an exceeding number of opportunities to discuss these things on camera but has refused every time: https://www.youtube.com/watch?v=dmjxuGlc06g&list=PLfzQB 1BVsbjhndiOpF5cjjPfszAqzGotQ&index=9

PCV (Pneumococcal) vaccine

According the CDC website: Vaccines are available that can help prevent pneumococcal disease(https://www.cdc.gov/pneumococcal/), which is any type of infection caused by *Streptococcus pneumoniae* bacteria. There are two kinds of pneumococcal vaccines available in the United States:

* Pneumococcal conjugate vaccine
* Pneumococcal polysaccharide vaccine

Pneumococcal conjugate vaccine is recommended for all babies and children younger than 2 years old, all adults 65 years or older, and people 2 through 64 years old with certain medical conditions. Pneumococcal polysaccharide vaccine is recommended for all adults 65 years or older, people 2 through 64 years old who are at increased risk for disease due to certain medical conditions, and adults 19 through 64 years old who smoke cigarettes.

PREVNAR: A Critical Review of a New Childhood Vaccine

"The safety and efficacy evaluations, and federal approval of Prevnar is laden with ethical questions. Many of the doctors directly involved in the testing and approval process appear to have significant conflicts of interest. The efficacy of the vaccine is questionable and safety testing has been terribly inadequate. There are no long-term studies (i.e. more than 5 years) of the chronic, debilitating and life threatening diseases that this vaccine may cause. The fact that the vaccine is bio-engineered by combining various types and portions of bacteria should require it to undergo considerable scrutiny. Assuming the vaccine has any efficacy at all, the need for universal vaccination needs to be reexamined in light of the small number of children who might be at risk from serious complications from pneumococcal disease."

http://www.whale.to/v/prevnar2.html

Pneumonia Vaccine Shown to Actually Increase Bacterial Infections It Is Supposed to Prevent

"Now it's being suggested that widespread use of the Prevnar vaccine is leading to other unforeseen consequences, like increases in bacterial infections and the emergence of antibiotic-resistant supergerms."

http://articles.mercola.com/sites/articles/archive/2012/05/22/pneumonia-vaccine-shown-to-actually-increase-bacterial-infections.aspx

There isn't a whole lot more to be able to discuss with this vaccine beyond these points at the moment – however in future versions of the book we hope to update it more.

Haemophilus influenzae type b or (Hib disease)

Haemophilus influenzae type b (Hib) is bacteria that commonly cause bacterial meningitis and pneumonia and the leading cause of other invasive diseases as septic arthritis (joint infection), epiglottitis (infection and swelling of the epiglottis), and cellulites (rapidly progressing skin infection which usually involves face, head, or neck). Pericardiatis (infection of the sac covering the heart) and osteomyelitis (bone infection) are less-common forms of invasive disease.

Haemophilus influenza (which includes Haemophilus influenza type B, or Hib), according to the CDC, is "a bacterium that can cause severe infection, occurring mostly in infants and children younger than five years of age. In spite of its name, Haemophilus influenza does not cause influenza (the 'flu')."

Work on an Hib vaccine began in 1968 by Porter W. Anderson, Jr., PhD, and David Smith, MD, which led to a 1975 trial that showed the vaccine worked in infants but not toddlers.

Smith founded a company to produce the vaccine when it was licensed in 1985 because no existing pharmaceutical company wanted to manufacture it. This HbPV polysaccharide vaccine was used until 1988. As of July 24, 2014, there are six Hib vaccines on the market (three for Hib only; one Hib/Hep B combination; one DTaP-IPV/Hib combination; and one meningococcal vaccine).

"VAERS received 29,747 reports after Hib vaccines; 5179 (17%) were serious, including 896 reports of deaths. Median age was 6 months (range 0-1022 months).

"Sudden infant death syndrome was the stated cause of death in 384 (51%) of 749 death reports with autopsy/death certificate records. The most common nondeath serious AE categories were neurologic (80; 37%), other noninfectious (46; 22%) (comprising mainly constitutional signs and symptoms); and gastrointestinal (39; 18%) conditions."

https://www.ncbi.nlm.nih.gov/m/pubmed/25598306/

Hib vaccine and diabetes...

"**The rise in diabetes, just one potential adverse effect, exceeds the benefit of the vaccine**, which has been estimated to prevent seven deaths and 7-26 cases of severe disability per 100 000 children immunised. Even the difference in cases of diabetes between the groups receiving four doses and one dose exceeds the mean expected benefit. Temporal changes in the incidence of diabetes do not explain the differences since there were an extra 31 cases of type 1 diabetes per 100 000 children aged 5-10, and the incidence of diabetes in this group had been stable for about 10 years before this.

"**Furthermore, sharp rises in diabetes have been recorded in the United States and the United Kingdom after the introduction of the haemophilus vaccine.** This also could be from a change in diet however."

https://www.ncbi.nlm.nih.gov/pmc/articles/PMC1116914/

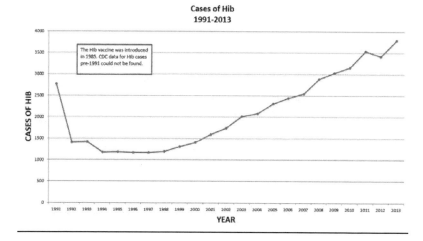

Cases of Hib
1991-2013

The Hib vaccine was introduced in 1985. CDC data for Hib cases pre-1991 could not be found.

CASES OF HIB

YEAR

Hib cases rise after vaccination begins.

Hib and Autism:

"Hypothesis: conjugate vaccines may predispose children to autism spectrum disorders."

"The first conjugate vaccine was approved for use in the U.S. in 1988 to protect infants and young children against the capsular bacteria Haemophilus influenzae type b (Hib). Since its introduction in the US, this vaccine has been approved in most developed countries, including Denmark and Israel where the vaccine was added to their national vaccine programs in 1993 and 1994, respectively. There have been marked increases in the reported prevalence of autism spectrum disorders (ASDs) among children in the U.S. beginning with birth cohorts in the late 1980s and in Denmark and Israel starting approximately 4-5 years later."

Please remember, however, that causation does not equal correlation. This is just food for thought.

Among numerous types of *H. influenzae*, the Hib vaccine covers only type b, despite its sole intention to reduce symptomatic and asymptomatic (disease-less) Hib carriage.

The introduction of the Hib vaccine has inadvertently shifted strain dominance towards other types of *H. influenzae* (types a through f). These types have been causing invasive disease of high severity and increasing incidence in adults in the era of Hib vaccination of children (see appendix for the scientific study, Item #4).

The general population is more vulnerable to the invasive disease now than it was prior to the start of the Hib vaccination campaign. Discriminating against children who are not vaccinated for Hib does not make any scientific sense in the era of non-type b *H. influenzae* disease.

The long story short is that while the Hib vaccine might prevent some cases of a certain type of Hib – the drawback is that it is creating a shift toward different strains – thus negating any benefits that vaccinating might have – not including the unknown number of adverse events it might have on an untold number of people.

HPV (Gardasil 5 and 9, Cervarix)

Gardasil is a vaccine developed by Merck to "protect against cervical cancer" under the slogan "one less". It is supposed to help protect against either 5 or 9 of the over 100 different strains of HPV that are out there (depending upon vaccine).

A glaringly large problem is that directly in all of the vaccine inserts for HPV it states, "This product has not been tested for carcinogenic or mutagenic properties, or for its effects on fertility."

I don't know about you – but if I were vaccinating for a disease of the reproductive system – I'd want to know what its effects on fertility were.

From 2006 to 2013, **VAERS alone** received over **20,000 adverse event reports** from the parents of girls – and this is just the number that has been reported. Many people I know – including my sister – collapsed in seizures in the doctor's office within seconds of the vaccine being administered – but were simply assured that "this was normal" – and was never reported to VAERS.

The other problem is – none of the HPV vaccines have ever been proven to prevent a single case of cervical cancer.

Don't take my word for it; listen to what Diane Harper, one of the lead researchers for the vaccine, and a whistleblower, has to say:

"It is silly to mandate vaccination of 11- to 12-year-old girls There also is not enough evidence gathered on side effects to know that safety is not an issue. This vaccine has not been tested in little girls for efficacy. At 11, these girls don't get cervical cancer – they won't know for 25 years if they will get

cervical cancer. ...To mandate now is simply to Merck's benefit, and only to Merck's benefit."

You can also consult her subsequent research that demonstrates *no* added protection above and beyond the Pap smear. Combined Pap smear and HPV vaccination have not been demonstrated to improve outcomes above Pap screening alone.

A recent review states, "Pap screening will still be required in vaccinated women hence HPV vaccination programs are not cost-effective, and may do more harm than good, in countries where regular Pap screening and surgery has already reduced the burden of this disease."

"At this time, protection against cervical intraepithelial neoplasia grade 2/3 (CIN 2/3) is 5 years for Gardasil and 8.4 years for Cervarix."
https://www.ncbi.nlm.nih.gov/pubmed/20670593

The cervical cancer diagnosis rate in the United States is 7.9/100,000. Given that only 5% of HPV infections progress to neoplasia (CIN) and that 91% of early stage cases resolve spontaneously within 36 months, with 70% of CIN 1 and 54% of CIN 2 cases doing the same within 12 months, using these pathologies as surrogate markers for cancer incidence represents a scientific shortcoming.

In a study just out, entitled, *Comparison of HPV prevalence between HPV-vaccinated and non-vaccinated young adult women (20-26 years)*, the perils of vaccination are revealed. Is the vaccine-based effect a desirable long-term outcome? This study would argue otherwise, concluding: *"...vaccinated women had a higher prevalence of nonvaccine high-risk types than unvaccinated women (61.5% vs. 39.7%, prevalence ratio 1.55, 95% CI 1.22-1.98)."*
http://www.abstractsonline.com/plan/ViewAbstract.aspx?mID=

162

Gardasil 9 is brought to us with a whopping dose of viral antigen, and a mind-crushing dose of aluminum – 1,500 mcg per 3 recommended doses. Also Gardasil 9, like many vaccines, was never tested against a true placebo. It was tested against the original Gardasil vaccine as a placebo – a violation of the gold standard of medical procedures of having a true placebo to compare against.

This is taken directly from the vaccine manufacturer's insert for Gardasil: "Across the clinical studies, 40 deaths (GARDASIL N = 21 or 0.1%; placebo N = 19 or 0.1%) were reported in 29,323 (GARDASIL N = 15,706; AAHS control N = 13,023, saline placebo N = 594) individuals (9- through 45-year-old girls and women; and 9- through 26-year-old boys and men). The events reported were consistent with events expected in healthy adolescent and adult populations."

40 deaths out of 29,323 study participants is 1 death for every 733 subjects.

Page7
https://www.fda.gov/downloads/BiologicsBloodVaccines/Vaccines/ApprovedProducts/UCM111263.pdf

What countries banned Gardasil?
A senior doctor in **Denmark**, where the administration of the Gardasil vaccine has been completely banned, has linked several chronic symptoms to the vaccination. Other countries to ban this vaccine and/or have current criminal lawsuits filed include **Japan**, **India**, **France**, and **Spain**.

"CONCLUSION: We documented here the evidence of the potential of the HPV vaccine to trigger a life-disabling autoimmune condition. The increasing number of similar reports of post HPV vaccine-linked autoimmunity and the uncertainty of long-term clinical benefits of HPV vaccination are a matter of public health that warrants further rigorous inquiry." https://www.ncbi.nlm.nih.gov/m/pubmed/23902317/

Adolescent Premature Ovarian Insufficiency Following Human Papillomavirus Vaccination

http://journals.sagepub.com/doi/full/10.1177/2324709614556129

In an unprecedented move, the American College of Pediatricians has issued a warning against a vaccine that has been approved by the FDA and CDC.

The College says that they are committed to the health and well-being of children, and due to their commitment to children's health, they feel that safety concerns regarding the Human Papillomavirus Vaccine Gardasil should be made public. The College says that in addition to concerning correlations between Gardasil and Premature Ovarian Failure, they are also concerned with the pre-release vaccine testing methods utilized by Gardasil maker Merck.

Pre-licensure safety trials for Gardasil used a placebo that contained polysorbate 80 as well as an aluminum adjuvant, which are both contained within the vaccine. Therefore, if either of these ingredients could cause ovarian dysfunction, an increase in amenorrhea probably would not have been detected. The College notes that the placebo-controlled trials were highly questionable due to the fact that the placebos were actually not placebos at all. http://circleofdocs.com/hpv-vaccine-american-college-of-pediatricians-issues-rare-warning-against-vaccine-due-to-premature-ovarian-failure/

Official statement...

http://www.acpeds.org/the-college-speaks/position-statements/health-issues/new-concerns-about-the-human-papillomavirus-vaccine

CONCLUSIONS:

In a population referred for symptoms of orthostatic intolerance and other symptoms consistent with autonomic dysfunction that began in close temporal association with a quadrivalent HPV vaccination, we identified a 60% prevalence of POTS. Further work is urgently needed to elucidate the potential for a causal link between the vaccine and circulatory abnormalities and to establish targeted treatment options for the affected patients.

https://www.ncbi.nlm.nih.gov/pubmed/25882168

Most recently, an oncology dietitian pointed out significant discrepancies in a new HPV vaccine effectiveness study published in the *Journal of Infectious Diseases*, which evaluated data from the National Health and Nutrition Examination Surveys (NHANES), 2003-2006 and 2007-2010.

The study pointed out that HPV vaccine uptake among young girls in the U.S. has been low but concluded that:

"Within four years of vaccine introduction, the vaccine-type HPV prevalence decreased among females aged 14–19 years despite low vaccine uptake. The estimated vaccine effectiveness was high."

In her article, Sharlene Bidini, RD, CSO, points out that the study's conclusion was based on 740 girls, of which only 358 were sexually active, and of those, only 111 had received at least one dose of the HPV vaccine.

In essence, the vast majority was unvaccinated, and nearly half were not at risk of HPV since they weren't sexually active.

"If the study authors were trying to determine vaccine effectiveness, why did they include the girls who had not received a single HPV shot or did not report having sex?" she writes.

"Table 1 from the journal article compares 1,363 girls, aged 14-19, in the pre-vaccine era (2003-2006) to all 740 girls in the post-vaccine era (2007-2010) regardless of sexual history or immunization status."

https://www.ncbi.nlm.nih.gov/pubmed/23785124

http://www.theonc.org/author.asp?section_id=2414

In the pre-vaccine era, an estimated 53 percent of sexually active girls between the ages of 14-19 had HPV. Between 2007 and 2010, the overall prevalence of HPV in the same demographic declined by just over 19 percent to an overall prevalence of nearly 43 percent.

As Bidini points out, this reduction in HPV prevalence can NOT be claimed to be due to the effectiveness of HPV vaccinations. On the contrary, the data clearly shows that it was the *unvaccinated* girls in this group that had the best outcome!

"In 2007-2010, the overall prevalence of HPV was 50 percent in the vaccinated girls (14-19 years), but only 38.6 percent in the unvaccinated girls of the same age.

"Therefore, HPV prevalence dropped 27.3 percent in the unvaccinated girls, but only declined by 5.8 percent in the vaccinated group. In four out of five different measures, the unvaccinated girls had a lower incidence of HPV," she writes.

Furthermore, in the single instance where unvaccinated girls had a 9.5 percent higher prevalence of HPV, a note stated that the relative standard error was greater than 30 percent, leading Bidini to suspect that "the confidence interval values must have been extremely wide. Therefore, this particular value is subject to too much variance and doesn't have much value."

Another fact hidden among the reported data was that among the 740 girls included in the post-vaccine era (2007-2010), the prevalence of high-risk, *non-vaccine types* of HPV *also* significantly declined, from just under 21 percent to just over 16 percent.

So, across the board, HPV of all types, whether included in the vaccine or not, declined. This points to a reduction in HPV prevalence that has *nothing* to do with vaccine coverage. Besides, vaccine uptake was very LOW to begin with.

All in all, one can conclude that there were serious design flaws involved in this study – whether intentional or not – leading the researchers to erroneously conclude that the vaccine effectiveness was "high." Clearly the effectiveness of the vaccine was *anything but* high, since the *unvaccinated* group fared far better across the board.

Many women are not aware that the HPV vaccine Gardasil might actually *increase* your risk of cervical cancer.

Initially, that information came straight from Merck and was presented to the FDA prior to approval. According to Merck's own research, if you have been exposed to HPV strains 16 or 18 prior to receipt of Gardasil vaccine, you could increase your risk of precancerous lesions, or worse, by 44.6 percent.

Other health problems associated with the Gardasil vaccine include immune-based inflammatory neurodegenerative disorders, suggesting that something is causing the immune system to overreact in a detrimental way – sometimes fatally.

- Between June 1, 2006 and December 31, 2008, there were 12,424 reported adverse events following Gardasil vaccination, including 32 deaths. The girls, who were on average 18 years old, died within two to 405 days after their last Gardasil injection

- Between May 2009 and September 2010, 16 additional deaths after Gardasil vaccination were reported. For that timeframe, there were also 789 reports of "serious" Gardasil adverse reactions, including 213 cases of permanent disability and 25 diagnosed cases of Guillain-Barré Syndrome

- Between September 1, 2010 and September 15, 2011, another 26 deaths were reported following HPV vaccination

- As of May 13, 2013, VAERS had received 29,686 reports of adverse events following HPV vaccinations, including 136 reports of death, as well as 922 reports of disability, and 550 life-threatening adverse events

https://www.fda.gov/ohrms/dockets/ac/06/briefing/2006-4222B3.pdf

http://www.medalerts.org/vaersdb/findfield.php?EVENTS=on&PAGENO=12&PERPAGE=10&ESORT=&REVERSESORT=&VAX=(HPV+HPV2+HPV4)&DIED=Yes

On February 28, 2013 the government watchdog group Judicial Watch announced it had filed a Freedom of Information Act (FOIA) lawsuit against the Department of Health and Human Services (DHHS) to obtain records from the Vaccine Injury Compensation Program (VICP) related to the HPV vaccine[7].

The lawsuit was filed in order to force the DHHS to comply with an earlier FOIA request, filed in November 2012, which had been ignored. As reported by WND.com:

"Judicial Watch wants all records relating to the VICP, any documented injuries or deaths associated with HPV vaccines and all records of compensation paid to the claimants following injury or death allegedly associated with the HPV vaccines... The number of successful claims made under the VICP to victims of HPV will provide further information about any dangers of the vaccine, including the number of well-substantiated cases of adverse reactions."

On March 20, Judicial Watch announced it had received the FOIA documents from the DDHS, which revealed that the National Vaccine Injury Compensation Program has awarded $5,877,710 to 49 victims for harm resulting from the HPV vaccine. According to the press release: *On March 12, 2013, The Health Resources and Services Administration (HRSA), an agency of HHS, provided Judicial Watch with documents revealing the following information:*

- *Only 49 of the 200 claims filed have been compensated for injury or death caused from the (HPV) vaccine. Of the 49 compensated claims, 47 were for injury caused from the (HPV) vaccine. The additional 2 claims were for death caused due to the vaccine.*

- *92 (nearly half) of the total 200 claims filed are still pending. Of those pending claims, 87 of the claims against the (HPV) vaccine were filed for injury. The remaining 5 claims were filed for death.*

- *59 claims have been dismissed outright by VICP. The alleged victims were not compensated for their claims against the HPV vaccine. Of the claims dismissed, 57 were for injuries, 2 were for deaths allegedly caused by the HPV vaccine.*

- *The amount awarded to the 49 claims compensated totaled 5,877,710.87 dollars. This amounts to approximately $120,000 per claim.*

"This new information from the government shows that the serious safety concerns about the use of Gardasil have been well-founded," said Judicial Watch President Tom Fitton. "Public health officials should stop pushing Gardasil on children."

http://www.judicialwatch.org/press-room/press-releases/jw-seeks-answers-to-payouts-made-to-victims-of-hpv-vaccines/

https://www.fda.gov/ohrms/dockets/ac/06/briefing/2006-4222B3.pdf

"We carried out a systematic review of HPV vaccine pre- and post-licensure trials to assess the evidence of their effectiveness and safety.

"We found that HPV vaccine clinical trials design, and data interpretation of both efficacy and safety outcomes, were largely inadequate.

*"Additionally, we note **evidence of selective reporting of results from clinical trials** (i.e., exclusion of vaccine efficacy figures related to study subgroups in which efficacy might be lower or even negative from peer-reviewed publications).*

"Given this, the widespread optimism regarding HPV vaccines long-term benefits appears to rest on a number of unproven assumptions (or such which are at odds with factual evidence) and significant misinterpretation of available data.

*"For example, **the claim that HPV vaccination will result in approximately 70% reduction of cervical cancers is made despite the fact that the clinical trials data have not demonstrated to date that the vaccines have actually prevented a single case of cervical cancer (let alone cervical cancer death), nor that the current overly optimistic surrogate marker-based extrapolations are justified.***

*"Likewise, **the notion that HPV vaccines have an impressive safety profile is only supported by highly flawed design of safety trials and is contrary to accumulating evidence from vaccine safety surveillance databases and case reports which continue to link HPV vaccination to serious adverse outcomes (including death and permanent disabilities).***

"We thus conclude that further reduction of cervical cancers might be best achieved by optimizing cervical screening (which carries no such risks) and targeting other factors of the disease rather than by the reliance on vaccines with questionable efficacy and safety profiles."

https://www.ncbi.nlm.nih.gov/pubmed/23016780

Flu Vaccine

This one I'm not going to spend a lot of time on – because honestly the none of the evidence that isn't slanted supports the use of a flu vaccine in any way. Year after year it's even admitted by the CDC to be an overall failure – and they don't even bring up the side effects that should be dealt with.

No studies are ever done before the release of it proving its effectiveness. It is however – the largest percentage of VAERS reports with adverse reactions and of settlements from injury.

Simply put as well – getting adequate levels of Vitamin D outperforms the flu vaccine every single year – of which there are no side effects and Vitamin D does not contain mercury unlike the flu vaccine – another plus. This webpage has links to the studies:
https://www.organicconsumers.org/news/vitamin-d-more-effective-flu-vaccine-study-says

Also people who get the flu vaccine – are not only more susceptible to other forms of infections – but also getting it more than one year in a row reduces its possible effectiveness even further.

Rather than take it from me – here are a few places that outline how the cost/benefit ratio from a flu shot does not support its use:

https://academic.oup.com/cid/article/54/12/1778/455098/Incr eased-Risk-of-Noninfluenza-Respiratory-Virus
http://www.cidrap.umn.edu/news-perspective/2013/03/study-getting-flu-shot-2-years-row-may-lower-protection
http://www.cidrap.umn.edu/news-perspective/2010/04/new-canadian-studies-suggest-seasonal-flu-shot-increased-h1n1-risk
http://www.naturalhealth365.com/flu-vaccine-respiratory-

infection-2157.html
http://articles.mercola.com/sites/articles/archive/2011/11/24/more-people-getting-flu-shots.aspx
And while I don't especially like this guy, his information here is solid:
http://www.naturalnews.com/024624_flu_the_shot.html

The worst part about the Flu vaccine – is that is recommended by the CDC for pregnant women – DESPITE it being stated clearly in the insert that "no controlled studies for safety in pregnant women have been done". The CDC once again is recommending an untested medical procedure be done on pregnant women – something that is completely unethical in every way.

To illustrate the point further – a recent study done (of course not by the manufacturers) **found an almost 800% rise in risk of spontaneous abortions to women who received the flu vaccine while pregnant:**
https://medium.com/@jbhandley/devastating-flu-vaccine-miscarriage-study-sparks-ridiculous-spin-c440bb14c867

http://kellybroganmd.com/rejecting-flu-vaccine-in-pregnancy/

Heavy Metals

Heavy metals are an utmost concern when it comes to overall wellbeing. Extremely low amounts are exceptionally toxic to numerous areas of the body – but especially the brain due to heavy metals having an affinity for fatty tissue.

Heavy metals carry a positive charge – and like a magnet – attract to a negative charge. Glutathione – one of the most powerful antioxidants in the human body – is powerfully electrically charged – and that's how it binds to and helps detoxify heavy metals and other toxins that carry a positive charge (nearly everything toxic carries a positive charge). Of course things with a negative charge can be toxic too – but the

173

positively charged ones by nature are usually the most worrisome.

Electrical signals in nerves are negatively charged – and thus attract heavy metals very readily as well. Electrical signals are found in the nerves and brain – and that's why there are different barriers to ensure that toxic substances do not get into these areas of the body.

This is the reason so many doctors and researchers raise such concerns over the levels of aluminum and mercury adjuvants in vaccines – their affinity for fatty and nervous tissue. (http://schizophreniahelpforyou.com/EXPERT%20PAPER%20-%20Geier%20-%20Internet%20File.pdf)

Each heavy metal carries with it a different "personality" if you will – and many toxicities can be diagnosed by comparing personality disorders/defects.

Back in the 1800s, hatters – that is people who make hats – used to line the felt rim of hats with mercury to keep it soft. The problem is – over time due to being around so much mercury – hatters had a tendency to go "crazy". Hence the term "As mad as a hatter". It was the inspiration behind "The Mad Hatter" in Alice in Wonderland – depicting the insanity that happened to hatters due to mercury toxicity.

Arsenic carries the personality of paranoia. Hitler was rumored to being slowly poisoned by an assassin with arsenic that caused him to become more and more paranoid over time – leading to many difficulties later on in the war.

Aluminum carries the personality of "hyperactivity" and inability to concentrate – or lack of focus. Many ADHD/ADD children are aluminum toxic – and many doctors speculate that the level of adjuvants in vaccines are contributing to the hyperactivity that children these days seem to be suffering from.

174

Lead carries the personality of "sedentary" – or lack of movement. Look at children who are lead toxic – they usually have profound gross and fine motor activity disabilities – and usually suffer from the lack of ability to speak due to the intense motor activity that is required to formulate sounds with the tongue (or even contemplate speaking).

This article lays out the latest research from Yale on how one piece of research found that individuals who got different vaccines were more likely to suffer from mental disorders than those who did not:
http://info.cmsri.org/the-driven-researcher-blog/vaccination-may-increase-risk-of-rare-psychiatric-childhood-disorders-study-finds

Here is also a neat study that backs up the one above as well:
https://medicalxpress.com/news/2017-10-immune-cells-behavioral.html

I would like to point out – this is only one study – and there are a LOT of variables – so we can't say that this is a for-sure thing. We can however say – it is something interesting to ponder due to the nature of heavy metals and the damage they can cause neurologically. It also is one of the only studies that has been done – because like I mentioned earlier – no true studies on vaccinated vs. unvaccinated individuals has been done for the most part. Especially not those measuring broad-spectrum possibilities when it comes to neurological disorders. Especially in light of the study showing activating T-Cells leads to behavioral changes above as well.

The other part of the problem is one that not many doctors are familiar with – as this field (although over 40 years old) is just finally gaining attention. It's the field of "Epigenetics".

I don't have time to go over this entire topic in this book – but the simple way to put it is that we have found that genetics are not static. They are changing second by second – and can be influenced by not only the world around a person – but by their experiences – and by their perception of said experiences.

The reason this is of such a concern is because DNA is strongly negatively charged. Remember when I said heavy metals have a strong affinity for negatively charged particles? Very few things carry a stronger negative charge in the body than DNA – making it a powerful magnet for heavy metals. Those who can understand epigenetic evolutionary ideas like myself find this especially concerning.

Aluminum (and many other heavy metals) have the tendency to interfere with protein production and assimilation – and your DNA is made of proteins.

http://www.vaclib.org/docs/alum/lukiw.htm

https://books.google.com/books?id=O8JkCSXX_14C&pg=PA118&lpg=PA118&dq=aluminum+inhibits+DNA&source=bl&ots=1hTy0EsJnX&sig=YywTqD7vCAj5O0lm2VpvU2MaqaA&hl=en&sa=X&ved=0ahUKEwiZn9f_-f_TAhVM5oMKHaWeAQA4ChDoAQglMAE#v=onepage&q=aluminum%20inhibits%20DNA&f=false

https://www.researchgate.net/publication/7621290_A_comet_assay_study_reveals_that_aluminum_induces_DNA_damage_and_inhibits_the_repair_of_radiation-induced_lesions_in_human_peripheral_blood_lymphocytes

https://springerplus.springeropen.com/articles/10.1186/s40064-016-3140-2

The list is quite extensive if you care to look for it.

The problem is, too, that since these young children are growing so much faster than adults – and their cells are dividing more rapidly – they are at much higher risk of the DNA/RNA/Gene Expression inhibitory properties of aluminum.

Heavy metals also help trap negative emotions into the DNA.

Here are a just a few articles on how memories can be passed through DNA:

https://www.theguardian.com/science/2015/aug/21/study-of-holocaust-survivors-finds-trauma-passed-on-to-childrens-genes

http://www.pbs.org/newshour/extra/daily_videos/can-trauma-be-passed-to-next-generation-through-dna/

http://www.huffingtonpost.com/dawson-church/genetic-tags-can-pass-tra_1_b_8068046.html

http://discovermagazine.com/2013/may/13-grandmas-experiences-leave-epigenetic-mark-on-your-genes

https://www.ncbi.nlm.nih.gov/pmc/articles/PMC3108177/

http://www.pbs.org/wgbh/nova/next/body/epigenetics-abuse/

There is also the topic of circumcision trauma becoming greater and greater over generations due the memories being passed down from previous traumas and circumcisions.

Very little is known about heavy metals and their ability to trap emotions so far – however many different doctors are recently addressing such topics. Here are just a few of many such ones:

http://www.breathing.com/articles/toxicmetals.htm

http://amalgam.org/376-2/

http://www.drrisley.com/html/heavymetal.html

https://books.google.com/books?id=NF_-g_vypK4C&pg=PA265&lpg=PA265&dq=toxic+metals+negative+emotions&source=bl&ots=I8vVneEkG1&sig=3DrCQTQirp1DRuE-M4yJpf9gdkk&hl=en&sa=X&ved=0ahUKEwjuvsXG-TAhVJbhQKHbpzCFkQ6AEIWzAJ#v=onepage&q=toxic%20metals%20negative%20emotions&f=false

These aren't perfect scholarly articles – but they do lay out the science behind how this would work and map it all out for you.

The reason I bring this up is because of the difficulty that usually exists when attempting to detoxify these metals. Until recently, it has been a very long, arduous, intensive, and painful process.

There are different types of heavy-metal chelation therapies, but each one has its limitations and side effects. Because chelation therapies do not distinguish between helpful ions such as calcium and other beneficial nutrients from heavy metals – it can be exceptionally difficult (and expensive – and painful – and dangerous) to undergo chelation therapy.

Most detoxification programs involve pulling the heavy metals out with numerous supplements and processes – then eliminating them from the body with other supplements and processes. The drawbacks of this are that it is expensive, time intensive, and often painful. That is because none of the standard methods easily render the toxins and heavy metals inert when they pull them out – so they are exceptionally toxic on the way out of the body – and any good practitioner who knows what they're doing attempts to address this as well.

I recently ran across a product however that does address all of these issues. It's called "Coseva Advanced TRS".

5 = 10

SPRAYS / DAY   IMPROV

In your body's ability
extract heavy metals
and other toxins

Advanced TRS is a nano-zeolite that is bound inside of a water molecule.

Zeolites have been used for centuries to help detoxify the body from different substances – but have attracted recent attention for their ability to be true chelators and bind heavy metals in "molecular cages" – rendering the heavy metals inert and harmless. This way they can be excreted safely without causing damage on the way out of the body and stressing the detoxification mechanism.

Also, due to the nature of zeolites – they do not bind to or interact with beneficial nutrients in the body. You can think of them as a "selective activated charcoal". When somebody ingests a toxic substance or overdoses on drugs, activated charcoal is usually given to the person to absorb the excess toxins so they can be safely excreted and not have negative effects on the body. The problem with activated charcoal is that it will bind to **BOTH** beneficial nutrients and toxic materials – this is just the nature of activated charcoal.

Advanced TRS selectively binds to toxic materials and does not bind to beneficial nutrients – so that's why I called it a "selective activated charcoal".

Standard zeolites only work in the upper digestive tract (where heavy metals get excreted from) – so the problem is #1 getting them out of where they are being stored and #2 getting them out of the body safely so they do not cause damage along the way to the digestive tract to be absorbed by the zeolites.

TRS solves this by making the zeolites nano-sized so they have an exceptional ratio of surface area to volume (making them able to absorb far more toxins than if they weren't) – and then bind them inside of a water molecule so they can pass the blood-brain barrier. Advanced TRS Zeolites do not interact with any part of the body or its processes that are beneficial to human life – making it an exceptional way to detoxify heavy metals without having to worry about all of the problems that come with standard heavy-metal detoxification protocols.

I'm not saying this is a medical treatment – or a replacement for a medical treatment of any kind.

I **AM** however saying that for anyone who would like to help reduce their heavy metal toxicity load safely (and easily, and affordably, and effectively), this would be the #1 product that should be on your list. I say this because I have tried all of the other ways except medical chelation therapy (after reading all of the downfalls, I personally decided I didn't want to try that option).

If you would like to learn more about this product, get some for yourself – head over to:

www.safeheavymetaldetox.com

However – after not only testing it with multiple people myself – and hearing some pretty amazing testimonies online – I decided to put it here because of the number of people it could possibly help.

It's just so much cheaper, faster, easier, and safer than any other way I've found to help lower toxic heavy metal loads – so I had to share it.

This is only in here for those that are looking for a safe way to help support the detox of adjuvants in the body after vaccination.

As a final note:

Throughout the entire book I stress this – and want this to be the last point of the book before the links to all of the studies:

Please, Please, **PLEASE –**

Always work WITH your doctor to find out what the best decision is for you and your family. They are a wealth of knowledge and (most) of them went into their profession to help children and their families. Without our doctor during the birthing process – well let's just say things probably wouldn't have turned out as well as they did.

No one person knows everything – that is why it is important to have an open discussion with your doctor at all times – that's what they are there for.

If your doctor is not open to discussing your concerns or answering your questions – then find a different doctor. That's all there is to it.

I of all people do not have all the answers by any means. This book simplified the topic of vaccines in the immune by so much it's not even funny.

That was also the point of this book, however. To come up with simple questions about concerns – and to try to provide exceedingly simplified statistics to help you get an understanding of what the true risks of medical procedures might be.

It is not to deter you from any medical procedure – it is to arm you most importantly with the questions to ask about them.

Answers are completely worthless without the question to go with them.

So be sure to discuss with your doctor – both the question **AND** the answer to that question until you feel you have been properly informed and educated on the topic enough

TO MAKE THE DECISION THAT IS RIGHT FOR YOU AND YOUR FAMILY.

To put the decision regarding your or your family's health –

solely into the hands of someone who bears none of the consequences of that decision –

is the greatest mistake a person could ever make.

We will also be creating a web page with the full downloadable abstracts to hundreds (if not thousands) of studies grouped by topic – so that you will always have access to the information you need to make the right decisions – for you.

Finally – I would like to point out that about 50% of the medical studies published today are false/fake:

https://www.ncbi.nlm.nih.gov/pmc/articles/PMC1182327/

https://www.theguardian.com/science/occams-corner/2013/sep/17/scientific-studies-wrong

I point this out not because I want you to NOT believe in medical literature – but because there is one simple thing you can do to overcome this.

Use common-sense judgment. When something seems blatantly obvious that there is a problem or something doesn't add up –

it's because it probably doesn't add up.

Use that common sense.

You don't need someone in a lab coat to come tell you when common sense isn't adding up.

Simple, Common, Sense

(although not so common anymore)

Studies

This is one of my favorite sites to download even more studies that what we have listed here in this book – we simply have not had time to cross reference and update all the new ones/duplicates in this book:

https://m.mediafire.com/folder/aj14280ch2qbp/Vaccine

Aluminum

Aluminum + fluoride = Aluminum fluoride

Aluminum fluoride + oxygen = Aluminum oxide

Aluminum oxide can bypass the blood brain barrier

https://www.psychologytoday.com/blog/iage/201407/is-dementia-caused-aluminum-through-fluoridation

https://www.psychologytoday.com/blog/iage/201407/fluoridation-and-dementia

Aluminum is in the following vaccines given to minors: DTaP, Pediarix (DTaP-Hepatitis B-Polio combination), Pentacle (DTaP-HIB-Polio combination), Hepatitis A, Hepatitis B, Homophiles influenza B (HIB), Human Papilloma Virus (HPV), and Pneumococcal vaccines

INGESTION VS INJECTION: "In healthy subjects, only 0.3% of orally administered aluminum is absorbed via the GI tract, and the kidneys effectively eliminate aluminum from the human body. **Only when the GI barrier is bypassed, such as by intravenous infusion or in the presence of advanced renal** dysfunction, does aluminum have the potential to accumulate. As an example, with intravenously infused aluminum, 40% is retained in adults and up to 75% is retained in neonates.

"If a significant aluminum load exceeds the body's excretory capacity, the excess is deposited in various tissues, including bone, brain, liver, heart, spleen, and muscle. This accumulation causes morbidity and mortality through various mechanisms."

http://emedicine.medscape.com/article/165315-overview

"In adults, aluminum exposure can lead to apparently age-related neurological deficits resembling Alzheimer's and has been linked to this disease and to the Guamanian variant, ALS-PDC. Similar outcomes have been found in animal models. In addition, injection of aluminum adjuvants in an attempt to model Gulf War syndrome and associated neurological deficits leads to an ALS phenotype in young male mice.

In young children, a highly significant correlation exists between the number of pediatric aluminum-adjuvant vaccines administered and the rate of autism spectrum disorders. Many of the features of aluminum-induced neurotoxicity may arise, in part, from autoimmune reactions, as part of the ASIA syndrome."

https://www.ncbi.nlm.nih.gov/m/pubmed/23609067/

"In young children, a highly significant correlation exists between the number of pediatric aluminum-adjuvanted vaccines administered and the rate of autism spectrum disorders. Many of the features of aluminum-induced neurotoxicity may arise, in part, from autoimmune reactions, as part of the ASIA syndrome."

http://link.springer.com/article/10.1007%2Fs12026-013-8403-1

"There is no evidence that human physiology is prepared for the challenge of biologically-reactive aluminium and it is naïve to assume that aluminium is a benign presence in the body. Aluminium is contributing to human disease and will continue to do so if its accumulation in the body is not checked or reversed."

http://www.bodycures.com/wp-content/uploads/2013/09/AluminiumAndMedicine_Christopher_Exley2008.pdf

"The aluminium content of a range of well known brands of infant formulas remains high and particularly so for a product designed for preterm infants and a soya-based product designed for infants with cow's milk intolerances and allergies. Recent research demonstrating the vulnerability of infants to early exposure to aluminium serves to highlight an urgent need to reduce the aluminium content of infant formulas to as low a level as is practically possible."

https://www.ncbi.nlm.nih.gov/pubmed/20807425?dopt=Abstract

"The application of the Hill's criteria to these data indicates that the correlation between Al in vaccines and ASD may be causal."

http://www.sciencedirect.com/science/article/pii/S0162013411002212

"aluminum in adjuvant form carries a risk for autoimmunity, long-term brain inflammation and associated neurological

191

complications and may thus have profound and widespread adverse health consequences."

http://www.ingentaconnect.com/content/ben/cmc/2011/0000 0018/00000017/art00011

"Aluminum-treated groups also showed significant motor neuron loss (35%) and increased numbers of astrocytes (350%) in the lumbar spinal cord. The findings suggest a possible role for the aluminum adjuvant in some neurological features associated with GWI and possibly an additional role for the combination of adjuvants."

http://link.springer.com/article/10.1385/NMM:9:1:83

"In summary, research evidence shows that increasing concerns about current vaccination practices may indeed be warranted. Because children may be most at risk of vaccine-induced complications, a rigorous evaluation of the vaccine-related adverse health impacts in the pediatric population is urgently needed."
https://www.ncbi.nlm.nih.gov/m/pubmed/22235057/

"Immunization with hepatitis B vaccine accelerates SLE-like disease in a murine model. Agmon-Levin N, et al. J Autoimmun. 2014. "Anxiety-like behavior was more pronounced among mice immunized with alum. In conclusion, herein we report that immunization with the HBVv (hepatitis b vaccine) aggravated kidney disease in an animal model of SLE. Immunization with either HBVv or alum affected bloodcounts, neurocognitive functions and brain gliosis. Our data support the concept that different component of vaccines may be linked with immune and autoimmune mediated adverse events."

https://www.ncbi.nlm.nih.gov/m/pubmed/25042822/

"The demonstrated neurotoxicity of aluminum hydroxide and its relative ubiquity as an adjuvant suggest that greater scrutiny by the scientific community is warranted."

https://www.ncbi.nlm.nih.gov/pmc/articles/PMC2819810/

"Aluminum adjuvant linked to Gulf War illness induces motor neuron death in mice. 2007 "Aluminum-treated groups also showed significant motor neuron loss (35%) and increased numbers of astrocytes (350%) in the lumbar spinal cord. The findings suggest a possible role for the aluminum adjuvant in some neurological features associated with GWI and possibly an additional role for the combination of adjuvants."

https://www.ncbi.nlm.nih.gov/pubmed/17114826

How aluminum, an intracellular ROS generator promotes hepatic and neurological diseases: the metabolic tale Cell Biology and Toxicity April 2013, Volume 29, Issue 2, pp. 75-84 https://link.springer.com/article/1... "Metal pollutants are a global health risk due to their ability to contribute to a variety of diseases. **Aluminum (Al), a ubiquitous environmental contaminant is implicated in anemia, Osteomalacia, hepatic disorder, and neurological disorder.** In this review, we outline how this intracellular generator of reactive oxygen species (ROS) triggers a metabolic shift towards lipogenesis in astrocytes and hepatocytes. **This Al-evoked phenomenon is coupled to diminished mitochondrial activity, anerobiosis, and the channeling of α-ketoacidosis towards anti-oxidant defense.** The resulting metabolic reconfiguration leads to fat accumulation and a reduction in ATP synthesis, characteristics that are common to numerous medical disorders. Hence, **the ability of Al toxicity to create an oxidative environment promotes dysfunctional metabolic processes in astrocytes and hepatocytes. These molecular events triggered by Al-induced ROS production are the potential mediators of brain and liver disorders.**"

"In particular, aluminum in adjuvant form carries a risk for autoimmunity, long-term brain inflammation and associated neurological complications and may thus have profound and widespread adverse health consequences. In our opinion, the possibility that vaccine benefits may have been overrated and the risk of potential adverse effects underestimated, has not been rigorously evaluated in the medical and scientific community" http://meerwetenoverfreek.nl/images/stories/Tomljenovic_Shaw-CMC-published.pdf

When assessing adjuvant toxicity in children, several key points ought to be considered:

1)   During prenatal and early postnatal development the brain is extremely vulnerable to neurotoxic insults;

2)   Aluminum is a neurotoxin and a strong immune stimulant. Hence, aluminum has all the necessary biochemical properties to induce neuro-immune diseases. Autism is one such disease. Namely, autism is characterized by dysfunctional immunity and abnormalities in brain function;

3)   In adult humans aluminum vaccine adjuvants have been linked to a variety of serious autoimmune and inflammatory conditions, yet children are regularly exposed to much higher amounts of aluminium from vaccines than adults;

4)   It is often incorrectly assumed that peripheral immune challenges (analogous to vaccinations) do not affect brain function. However, it is now clearly established that there is a cross-talk between the nervous and the immune system. It is also demonstrated that this cross-talk plays a crucial role in both immunoregulation as well as brain function. In turn, perturbations of the neuro-immune regulatory system have been demonstrated in many autoimmune diseases and are thought to be driven by a hyperactive immune response;

5) The same components of the neuro-immune regulatory system that have key roles in both brain development and immune function are heavily affected by aluminum adjuvants http://www.prweb.com/releases/2012/1/prweb9146755.htm

A histological study of toxic effects of aluminium sulfate on rat hippocampus.

https://www.ncbi.nlm.nih.gov/pubmed/25314162

Adverse events following immunization with vaccines containing adjuvants.

https://www.ncbi.nlm.nih.gov/pubmed/23576057

Administration of aluminium to neonatal mice in vaccine-relevant amounts is associated with adverse long term neurological outcomes

http://www.sciencedirect.com/science/article/pii/S0162013413001773

ALUMINIUM AND MEDICINE

http://www.bodycures.com/wp-content/uploads/2013/09/AluminiumAndMedicine_ChristopherExley2008.pdf

Aluminum adjuvant linked to gulf war illness induces motor neuron death in mice

http://link.springer.com/article/10.1385/NMM:9:1:83

Aluminum Adjuvant in Vaccines Causes Risk to Children According to New Journal Report

http://www.prweb.com/releases/2012/1/prweb9146755.htm

Aluminum Adjuvant Injection Experiment #3: 550mcg/kg

http://vaccinepapers.org/aluminum-experiments-part3/

195

Aluminium, carbonyls and cytokines in human nipple aspirate fluids: Possible relationship between inflammation, oxidative stress and breast cancer microenvironment

https://www.ncbi.nlm.nih.gov/pubmed/23916117

Aluminum content of parenteral nutrition in neonates: measured versus calculated levels

https://www.ncbi.nlm.nih.gov/pubmed/20038851

Aluminum hydroxide injections lead to motor deficits and motor neuron degeneration

https://www.ncbi.nlm.nih.gov/pubmed/19740540

Aluminium impairs the glutamate-nitric oxide-cGMP pathway in cultured neurons and in rat brain in vivo: molecular mechanisms and implications for neuropathology.

https://www.ncbi.nlm.nih.gov/pubmed/11709215

Aluminum-Induced Entropy in Biological Systems: Implications for Neurological Disease

https://www.hindawi.com/journals/jt/2014/491316/

Aluminum induces inflammatory and proteolytic alterations in human monocytic cell line

https://www.ncbi.nlm.nih.gov/pubmed/26421828

Aluminum is a potential environmental factor for Crohn's disease induction: extended hypothesis.

https://www.ncbi.nlm.nih.gov/pubmed/17804561

Aluminium overload after 5 years in skin biopsy following post-vaccination with subcutaneous pseudolymphoma.

https://www.ncbi.nlm.nih.gov/pubmed/22425036

Aluminum stimulates uptake of non-transferrin bound iron and transferrin bound iron in human glial cells.

https://www.ncbi.nlm.nih.gov/pubmed/17376497

Aluminum Vaccine Adjuvants: Are they Safe?

**http://www.ingentaconnect.com/content/ben/cmc/2011/000
00018/00000017/art00011**

Aluminum in the central nervous system (CNS): toxicity in humans and animals, vaccine adjuvants, and autoimmunity.

https://www.ncbi.nlm.nih.gov/m/pubmed/23609067/

Aluminum hydroxide injections lead to motor deficits and motor neuron degeneration

https://www.ncbi.nlm.nih.gov/pmc/articles/PMC2819810/

Aluminum Toxicity

http://emedicine.medscape.com/article/165315-overview

Analysis of aluminium content and iron homeostasis in nipple aspirate fluids from healthy women and breast cancer-affected patients

https://www.ncbi.nlm.nih.gov/pubmed/21337589

Are there negative CNS impacts of aluminum adjuvants used in vaccines and immunotherapy?

https://www.ncbi.nlm.nih.gov/pubmed/25428645

Biopersistence and brain translocation of aluminum adjuvants of vaccines

http://journal.frontiersin.org/article/10.3389/fneur.2015.00004
/full

Circulating levels of metals are related to carotid atherosclerosis in elderly

https://www.ncbi.nlm.nih.gov/pubmed/22178028

Curcumin attenuates aluminum-induced functional neurotoxicity in rats.

https://www.ncbi.nlm.nih.gov/pubmed/19376155

Debunking Aluminum Adjuvant, Part 2: FDA's Flawed Study of Al Adjuvant Toxicity (The Mitkus study)

http://vaccinepapers.org/debunking-aluminum-adjuvant-part-2/

Do aluminum vaccine adjuvants contribute to the rising prevalence of autism?

http://www.sciencedirect.com/science/article/pii/S0162013411002212

Effect of routine vaccination on aluminum and essential element levels in preterm infants.

https://www.ncbi.nlm.nih.gov/pubmed/23856981

Effect of aluminium on migration of oestrogen unresponsive MDA-MB-231 human breast cancer cells in culture.

https://www.ncbi.nlm.nih.gov/pubmed/26365320

Effects of vitamin E against aluminum neurotoxicity in rats.

https://www.ncbi.nlm.nih.gov/pubmed/16545059

Effects of aluminum ingestion on spontaneous motor activity of mice.

https://www.ncbi.nlm.nih.gov/pubmed/2755419

Highly delayed systemic translocation of aluminum-based adjuvant in CD1 mice following intramuscular injections.

https://www.ncbi.nlm.nih.gov/pubmed/26384437

How aluminum, an intracellular ROS generator promotes hepatic and neurological diseases: the metabolic tale

https://link.springer.com/article/10.1007%2Fs10565-013-9239-0

In vivo absorption of aluminium-containing vaccine adjuvants using 26Al.

https://www.ncbi.nlm.nih.gov/pubmed/9302736

Insight into the cellular fate and toxicity of aluminium adjuvants used in clinically approved human vaccinations.

https://www.ncbi.nlm.nih.gov/pubmed/27515230

Is Dementia Caused By Aluminum Through Fluoridation?

https://www.psychologytoday.com/blog/iage/201407/is-dementia-caused-aluminum-through-fluoridation

Lessons from macrophagic myofasciitis: towards definition of a vaccine adjuvant-related syndrome

https://www.ncbi.nlm.nih.gov/pubmed/12660567

Link between Aluminum and the Pathogenesis of Alzheimer's Disease: The Integration of the Aluminum and Amyloid Cascade Hypotheses.

https://www.ncbi.nlm.nih.gov/pubmed/21423554

Long-term follow-up of cognitive dysfunction in patients with aluminum hydroxide-induced macrophagic myofasciitis (MMF).

https://www.ncbi.nlm.nih.gov/pubmed/22099155

Long-term persistence of vaccine-derived aluminum hydroxide is associated with chronic cognitive dysfunction

https://www.ncbi.nlm.nih.gov/pubmed/19748679

Macrophagic myofasciitis lesions assess long-term persistence of vaccine-derived aluminium hydroxide in muscle

https://www.ncbi.nlm.nih.gov/pubmed/11522584

Macrophagic myofasciitis lesions assess long-term persistence of vaccine-derived aluminium hydroxide in muscle.

https://www.ncbi.nlm.nih.gov/pubmed/11522584

Mechanisms of aluminum adjuvant toxicity and autoimmunity in pediatric populations.

https://www.ncbi.nlm.nih.gov/m/pubmed/22235057/

Metabolism and possible health effects of aluminum.

https://www.ncbi.nlm.nih.gov/pmc/articles/PMC1474689/

Nanomolar aluminum induces expression of the inflammatory systemic biomarker
C-reactive protein (CRP) in human brain microvessel endothelial cells (hBMECs)

https://www.ncbi.nlm.nih.gov/pubmed/26265215

Nanomolar aluminum induces pro-inflammatory and pro-apoptotic gene expression in human brain cells in primary culture

https://www.ncbi.nlm.nih.gov/pubmed/15961160

Non-linear dose-response of aluminium hydroxide adjuvant particles:
Selective low dose neurotoxicity

http://vaccinepapers.org/wp-content/uploads/Non-linear-dose-response-of-aluminium-hydroxide-adjuvant-particles-Selective-low-dose-neurotoxicity.pdf

Non-invasive therapy to reduce the body burden of aluminium in Alzheimer's disease.

https://www.ncbi.nlm.nih.gov/pubmed/16988476

Protective effect of curcumin (*Curcuma longa*), against aluminium toxicity:
Possible behavioral and biochemical alterations in rats

https://www.ncbi.nlm.nih.gov/pubmed/19616038

Selective induction of IL-6 by aluminum-induced oxidative stress can be prevented by selenium.

https://www.ncbi.nlm.nih.gov/pubmed/23219369

Synergistic effects of iron and aluminum on stress-related gene expression in primary human neural cells.

https://www.ncbi.nlm.nih.gov/pubmed/16308480

Systematic review of potential health risks posed by pharmaceutical, occupational and consumer exposures to metallic and nanoscale aluminum, aluminum oxides, aluminum hydroxide and its soluble salts.

https://www.ncbi.nlm.nih.gov/pubmed/25233067

The disruption of l-carnitine metabolism by aluminum toxicity and oxidative
stress promotes dyslipidemia in human astrocytic and hepatic cells

https://www.ncbi.nlm.nih.gov/pubmed/21439360

There is (still) too much aluminium in infant formulas

https://www.ncbi.nlm.nih.gov/pubmed/20807425?dopt=Abst
ract

Unequivocal identification of
intracellular aluminium adjuvant in a
monocytic THP-1 cell line

https://www.nature.com/articles/srep06287

Quercetin Protects Against Chronic Aluminum-Induced
Oxidative Stress and Ensuing Biochemical, Cholinergic, and
Neurobehavioral Impairments in Rats

http://link.springer.com/article/10.1007/s12640-012-9351-6

Vaccine Aluminum Travels Into The Brain
http://vaccinepapers.org/vaccine-aluminum-travels-to-the-
brain/

Vitamin E protects the brain against oxidative injury stimulated
by excessive aluminum intake.

https://www.ncbi.nlm.nih.gov/pubmed/9891850

AUTISM

A comparison of temporal trends in United States autism
prevalence to trends in suspected environmental factors

https://www.ncbi.nlm.nih.gov/pmc/articles/PMC4177682/

A case series of children with apparent mercury toxic encephalopathies manifesting with clinical symptoms of regressive autistic disorders.

https://www.ncbi.nlm.nih.gov/pubmed/17454560

A comprehensive review of mercury provoked autism.

https://www.ncbi.nlm.nih.gov/pubmed/19106436

A possible central mechanism in autism spectrum disorders, part 1.

https://www.ncbi.nlm.nih.gov/pubmed/19043938

A Study of Nuclear Transcription Factor-Kappa B in Childhood Autism

https://www.ncbi.nlm.nih.gov/pmc/articles/PMC3090385/

Aberrant NF-KappaB Expression in Autism Spectrum Condition: A Mechanism for Neuroinflammation

https://www.ncbi.nlm.nih.gov/pmc/articles/PMC3098713/

A positive association found between autism prevalence and childhood vaccination uptake across the U.S. population.

https://www.ncbi.nlm.nih.gov/pubmed/21623535

A case series of children with apparent mercury toxic encephalopathies manifesting with clinical symptoms of regressive autistic disorders.

https://www.ncbi.nlm.nih.gov/pubmed/17454560

An investigation of porphyrinuria in Australian children with autism

https://www.ncbi.nlm.nih.gov/pubmed/18704827

A Review of the Differences in Developmental, Psychiatric, and Medical Endophenotypes Between Males and Females with Autism Spectrum Disorder

https://www.ncbi.nlm.nih.gov/pmc/articles/PMC4490156/

Abnormal measles-mumps-rubella antibodies and CNS autoimmunity in children with autism.

https://www.ncbi.nlm.nih.gov/pubmed/12145534

Abnormal immune response to brain tissue antigen in the syndrome of autism.

https://www.ncbi.nlm.nih.gov/pubmed/6182806

Adverse Events following 12 and 18 Month Vaccinations: a Population-Based, Self-Controlled Case Series Analysis

http://journals.plos.org/plosone/article?id=10.1371/journal.pone.0027897

Altered urinary porphyrins and mercury exposure as biomarkers for autism severity in Egyptian children with autism spectrum disorder

https://link.springer.com/article/10.1007/s11011-016-9870-6

Ancestry of pink disease (infantile acrodynia) identified as a risk factor for autism spectrum disorders.

https://www.ncbi.nlm.nih.gov/pubmed/21797771

Assessment of Infantile Mineral Imbalances in Autism Spectrum Disorders (ASDs)

https://www.ncbi.nlm.nih.gov/pmc/articles/PMC3863885/

Autism spectrum disorder prevalence and proximity to industrial facilities releasing arsenic, lead or mercury http://www.sciencedirect.com/science/article/pii/S0048969715303727

Autism: a novel form of mercury poisoning

https://www.ncbi.nlm.nih.gov/pubmed/11339848?dopt=Abstract

Autism: A form of lead and mercury toxicity

http://www.sciencedirect.com/science/article/pii/S1382668914002415

B-Lymphocytes from a Population of Children with Autism Spectrum Disorder and Their Unaffected Siblings Exhibit Hypersensitivity to Thimerosal

https://www.hindawi.com/journals/jt/2013/801517/

Blood Levels of Mercury Are Related to Diagnosis of Autism: A Reanalysis of an Important Data Set

http://journals.sagepub.com/doi/abs/10.1177/0883073807307111

Blood–brain barrier and intestinal epithelial barrier alterations in autism spectrum disorders

https://molecularautism.biomedcentral.com/articles/10.1186/s13229-016-0110-z

Correlations Between Gene Expression and Mercury Levels in Blood of Boys With and Without Autism

https://www.ncbi.nlm.nih.gov/pmc/articles/PMC3006666/

Commentary--Controversies surrounding mercury in vaccines: autism denial as impediment to universal immunization

https://www.ncbi.nlm.nih.gov/pubmed/25377033

Cultured lymphocytes from autistic children and non-autistic siblings up-regulate heat shock protein RNA in response to thimerosal challenge.

https://www.ncbi.nlm.nih.gov/pubmed/16870260

Detection and sequencing of measles virus from peripheral mononuclear cells from patients with inflammatory bowel disease and autism.

https://www.ncbi.nlm.nih.gov/pubmed/10759242

Developmental Regression and Mitochondrial Dysfunction in a Child With Autism

http://journals.sagepub.com/doi/abs/10.1177/0883073806021 0021401

Developmental Regression and Mitochondrial Dysfunction in a Child With Autism

http://journals.sagepub.com/doi/abs/10.1177/0883073806021 0021401

Do aluminum vaccine adjuvants contribute to the rising prevalence of autism?

http://omsj.org/reports/tomljenovic%202011.pdf

Does thimerosal or other mercury exposure increase the risk for autism? A review of current literature

https://www.ncbi.nlm.nih.gov/pubmed/20628442

Empirical Data Confirm Autism Symptoms Related to Aluminum and Acetaminophen Exposure

http://www.mdpi.com/1099-4300/14/11/2227

Enrichment of Elevated Plasma F_{2t}-Isoprostane Levels in Individuals with Autism Who Are Stratified by Presence of Gastrointestinal Dysfunction

http://journals.plos.org/plosone/article?id=10.1371/journal.po ne.0068444

Epidemiology of autism spectrum disorder in Portugal: prevalence, clinical characterization, and medical conditions
http://adventuresinautism.com/images/VivaPortugal.pdf

Etiology of autism spectrum disorders: Genes, environment, or both?
http://www.oapublishinglondon.com/article/1368

Exposure to mercury and aluminum in early life: developmental vulnerability as a modifying factor in neurologic and immunologic effects

https://www.ncbi.nlm.nih.gov/pubmed/25625408

Evidence of toxicity, oxidative stress, and neuronal insult in autism.

https://www.ncbi.nlm.nih.gov/pubmed/17090484

Hepatitis B vaccination of male neonates and autism diagnosis, NHIS 1997-2002.

https://www.ncbi.nlm.nih.gov/pubmed/21058170

Hepatitis B triple series vaccine and developmental disability in US children aged 1–9 years

http://www.tandfonline.com/doi/abs/10.1080/0277224070180 6501

Hypothesis: conjugate vaccines may predispose children to autism spectrum disorders

https://www.ncbi.nlm.nih.gov/pubmed/21993250

Identification of Unique Gene Expression Profile in Children with Regressive Autism Spectrum Disorder (ASD) and Ileocolitis

http://journals.plos.org/plosone/article?id=10.1371/journal.po ne.0058058

Increased risk of developmental neurologic impairment after high exposure to thimerosal-containing vaccine in first month of life.

http://mercury-freedrugs.org/docs/00mmdd_EISAbstractSubmission_Increased RiskOfDevelopmentalNeurologicImpairmentAfterHighExposureT oThimerosal-containingVaccine_.pdf

Induction of metallothionein in mouse cerebellum and cerebrum with low-dose thimerosal injection.

https://www.ncbi.nlm.nih.gov/pubmed/19357975

Influence of pediatric vaccines on amygdala growth and opioid ligand binding in rhesus macaque infants: A pilot
http://www.ane.pl/pdf/7020.pdf

Infection, vaccines and other environmental triggers of autoimmunity.

https://www.ncbi.nlm.nih.gov/pubmed/16126512

Impact of environmental factors on the prevalence of autistic disorder after 1979 http://www.academicjournals.org/journal/JPHE/article-abstract/C98151247042

Interplay of glia activation and oxidative stress formation in fluoride and aluminium exposure.

https://www.ncbi.nlm.nih.gov/pubmed/25577494

Large brains in autism: the challenge of pervasive abnormality.

https://www.ncbi.nlm.nih.gov/pubmed/16151044

Metabolic biomarkers of increased oxidative stress and impaired methylation capacity in children with autism

http://ajcn.nutrition.org/content/80/6/1611.full#aff-1

Mercury, Lead, and Zinc in Baby Teeth of Children with Autism Versus Controls

http://www.tandfonline.com/doi/abs/10.1080/15287390601172080

Mercury and autism: accelerating evidence?

https://www.ncbi.nlm.nih.gov/pubmed/16264412

Mitochondrial dysfunction in autism spectrum disorders: a systematic review and meta-analysis

https://www.scribd.com/doc/220807175/132-Research-Papers-Supporting-the-Vaccine-Autism-Link

MMR vaccination and febrile seizures: evaluation of susceptible subgroups and long-term prognosis.

https://www.ncbi.nlm.nih.gov/pubmed/15265850

Neurodevelopment outcomes in children exposed to organic mercury from multiple sources in a tin-ore mine environment in Brazil

https://www.ncbi.nlm.nih.gov/pubmed/25425160

Neuroglial activation and neuroinflammation in the brain of patients with autism.

https://www.ncbi.nlm.nih.gov/pubmed/15546155

Neurological adverse events associated with vaccination.

https://www.ncbi.nlm.nih.gov/pubmed/12045734

Oxidative Stress in Autism: Elevated Cerebellar 3-nitrotyrosine Levels

http://thescipub.com/html/10.3844/ajbbsp.2008.73.84

Oxidative stress in autism.

https://www.ncbi.nlm.nih.gov/pubmed/16766163

Pilot comparative study on the health of vaccinated and unvaccinated 6- to 12-year-old U.S. children

http://www.cmsri.org/wp-content/uploads/2017/05/MawsonStudyHealthOutcomes5.8.2017.pdf

Porphyrinuria in Korean children with autism: correlation with oxidative stress.

https://www.ncbi.nlm.nih.gov/pubmed/20391113

Possible immunological disorders in autism: concomitant autoimmunity and immune tolerance.

https://www.ncbi.nlm.nih.gov/pubmed/17974154

Preterm birth, vaccination and neurodevelopmental disorders: a cross-sectional study of 6- to 12-year-old vaccinated and unvaccinated children

http://www.oatext.com/Preterm-birth-vaccination-and-neurodevelopmental-disorders-a-cross-sectional-study-of-6-to-12-year-old-vaccinated-and-unvaccinated-children.php#Article

Reduced levels of mercury in first baby haircuts of autistic children.

https://www.ncbi.nlm.nih.gov/pubmed/12933322

Risk factors for autistic regression: results of an ambispective cohort study.

https://www.ncbi.nlm.nih.gov/pubmed?term=Risk%20Factors%20for%20Autistic%20Regression%3A%20Results%20of%20an%20Ambispective%20Cohort%20Study.

Serological association of measles virus and human herpesvirus-6 with brain autoantibodies in autism.

https://www.ncbi.nlm.nih.gov/pubmed/9756729

Slow CCL2-dependent translocation of biopersistent particles from muscle to brain

http://bmcmedicine.biomedcentral.com/articles/10.1186/1741-7015-11-99

Sorting Out the Spinning of Autism: Heavy Metals and the Question of Incidence

https://www.ncbi.nlm.nih.gov/labs/articles/20628440/

The Neurobiology of Autism

http://onlinelibrary.wiley.com/doi/10.1111/j.1750-3639.2007.00102.x/full

The potential importance of steroids in the treatment of autistic spectrum disorders and other disorders involving mercury toxicity.

https://www.ncbi.nlm.nih.gov/pubmed/15780490

Thimerosal and autism? A plausible hypothesis that should not be dismissed.

https://www.ncbi.nlm.nih.gov/pubmed/15082108

Thimerosal exposure in infants and neurodevelopmental disorders: an assessment of computerized medical records in the Vaccine Safety Datalink.

https://www.ncbi.nlm.nih.gov/pubmed/18482737

Toxic Metals and Essential Elements in Hair and Severity of Symptoms among Children with Autism

https://www.ncbi.nlm.nih.gov/pmc/articles/PMC3484795/

Thioredoxin: a novel, independent diagnosis marker in children with autism

https://www.ncbi.nlm.nih.gov/pubmed/25433158

Theoretical aspects of autism: Causes—A review

http://www.tandfonline.com/doi/abs/10.3109/1547691X.2010.545086

Topoisomerases facilitate transcription of long genes linked to autism

http://www.nature.com/nature/journal/v501/n7465/full/nature12504.html

Transcriptome analysis reveals dysregulation of innate immune response genes and neuronal activity-dependent genes in autism.

https://www.ncbi.nlm.nih.gov/pubmed/25494366

What's going on? The question of time trends in autism.

https://www.ncbi.nlm.nih.gov/pmc/articles/PMC1497666/

What is regressive autism and why does it occur? Is it the consequence of multi-systemic dysfunction affecting the elimination of heavy metals and the ability to regulate neural temperature?

https://www.ncbi.nlm.nih.gov/pmc/articles/PMC3364648/#!po=2.00000

Fluoride

(This list is very incomplete because the list is so long and very easy to find more such studies – and suggest people head to www.pubmed.gov and type in "Fluoride toxicity" for hundreds of more studies)

A cross-sectional study to assess the intelligence quotient (IQ) of school going children aged 10-12 years in villages of Mysore district, India with different fluoride levels.

https://www.ncbi.nlm.nih.gov/pubmed/26381633

A correlation between Serum Vitamin, Acetylcholinesterase Activity and IQ in Children with Excessive Endemic Fluoride exposure in Rajasthan, India
http://www.isca.in/MEDI_SCI/Archive/v1/i3/2.ISCA-IRJMedS-2013-010.pdf

A comparative analysis of the results of multiple tests in patients with chronic industrial fluorosis

http://www.fluoridealert.org/wp-content/uploads/duan-1995.pdf
A Study of the IQ Levels of Four to Seven-year-old Children in High Fluoride Areas
https://www.researchgate.net/publication/237647669_A_Study_of_the_IQ_Levels_of_Four_to_Seven-year-old_Children_in_High_Fluoride_Areas

Adverse Effects of High Concentrations of Fluoride on Characteristics of the Ovary and Mature Oocyte of Mouse
https://www.ncbi.nlm.nih.gov/pmc/articles/PMC4460091/

Alimentary fluoride intake in preschool children

https://www.ncbi.nlm.nih.gov/pmc/articles/PMC3201925/

Are fluoride levels in drinking water associated with hypothyroidism prevalence in England? A large observational study of GP practice data and fluoride levels in drinking water
http://jech.bmj.com/content/early/2015/02/09/jech-2014-204971?sid=387994a1-4d28-493a-bef6-8fdf845ecbb0

Arsenic and fluoride exposure in drinking water: children's IQ and growth in Shanyin county, Shanxi province, China.
https://www.ncbi.nlm.nih.gov/pubmed/17450237
ASSESSMENT OF GROUNDWATER QUALITY WITH SPECIAL REFERENCE TO FLUORIDE AND ITS IMPACT ON IQ OF SCHOOLCHILDREN IN SIX VILLAGES OF THE MUNDRA REGION, KACHCHH, GUJARAT, INDIA

http://fluoridealert.org/wp-content/uploads/trivedi-2012.pdf

Association of lifetime exposure to fluoride and cognitive functions in Chinese children: a pilot study.

https://www.ncbi.nlm.nih.gov/pubmed/25446012

Comparative Assessment of Intelligence Quotient among Children Living in High and Low Fluoride Areas of Kutch, India-a Pilot Study

https://www.ncbi.nlm.nih.gov/pmc/articles/PMC4441911/

Chronic Fluoride Toxicity: Dental Fluorosis

https://www.ncbi.nlm.nih.gov/pmc/articles/PMC3433161/

Community water fluoridation predicts increase in age-adjusted incidence and prevalence of diabetes in 22 states from 2005 and 2010

https://www.ncbi.nlm.nih.gov/pmc/articles/PMC5116242/

Decreased intelligence in children and exposure to fluoride and arsenic in drinking water.
https://www.ncbi.nlm.nih.gov/pubmed/18038039

Dental fluorosis and urinary fluoride concentration as a reflection of fluoride exposure and its impact on IQ level and BMI of children of Laxmisagar, Simlapal Block of Bankura District, W.B., India.

https://www.ncbi.nlm.nih.gov/pubmed/26960765

Developmental Fluoride Neurotoxicity: A Systematic Review and Meta-Analysis
https://ehp.niehs.nih.gov/1104912/
Effect of fluoride in drinking water on children's intelligence in high and low fluoride areas of Delhi

http://www.jiaphd.org/article.asp?issn=2319-5932;year=2015;volume=13;issue=2;spage=116;epage=121;aulast=Kundu

215

Exposure to fluoridated water and attention deficit
hyperactivity disorder prevalence among children and
adolescents in the United States: an ecological association

http://ehjournal.biomedcentral.com/articles/10.1186/s12940-
015-0003-1

Effect of fluoride exposure on the intelligence of school children
in Madhya Pradesh, India

https://www.ncbi.nlm.nih.gov/pmc/articles/PMC3409983/

EFFECT OF FLUORIDE IN DRINKING WATER
ON CHILDREN'S INTELLIGENCE
http://www.fluorideresearch.org/362/files/FJ2003_v36_n2_p84
-94.pdf
Effects of endemic fluoride poisoning on the intellectual
development of children in Baotou
https://www.researchgate.net/publication/291795479_Effects_
of_endemic_fluoride_poisoning_on_the_intellectual_developm
ent_of_children_in_Baotou

[Effects of high iodine and high fluorine on children's
intelligence and the metabolism of iodine and fluorine].
https://www.ncbi.nlm.nih.gov/pubmed/7859263

Effect of High Water Fluoride Concentration on the Intellectual
Development of Children in Makoo/Iran

https://www.ncbi.nlm.nih.gov/pmc/articles/PMC3484826/

Effect of fluoride exposure on the intelligence of school children
in Madhya Pradesh, India.

https://www.ncbi.nlm.nih.gov/pubmed/22865964

Effect of fluoride exposure on Intelligence Quotient (IQ) among 13-15 year old school children of known endemic area of fluorosis, Nalgonda District, Andhra Pradesh. http://fluoridealert.org/wp-content/uploads/sudhir-2009.pdf

Fluoride and aluminum release from restorative materials using ion chromatography

https://www.ncbi.nlm.nih.gov/pmc/articles/PMC3928768/

Fluoride and Arsenic Exposure Impairs Learning and Memory and Decreases mGluR5 Expression in the Hippocampus and Cortex in Rats

https://www.ncbi.nlm.nih.gov/pmc/articles/PMC3997496/

Fluoride and IQ deficits – A Research and Policy Review http://www.valparaisoutilities.org/DocumentCenter/View/377

Fluoride in drinking water and diet: the causative factor of chronic kidney diseases in the North Central Province of Sri Lanka

https://www.ncbi.nlm.nih.gov/pmc/articles/PMC4491063/

Fluoride induces oxidative damage and SIRT1/autophagy through ROS-mediated JNK signaling

https://www.ncbi.nlm.nih.gov/pmc/articles/PMC4684823/

High fluoride and low calcium levels in drinking water is associated with low bone mass, reduced bone quality and fragility fractures in sheep

https://www.ncbi.nlm.nih.gov/pmc/articles/PMC4048471/

Impact of fluoride on neurological development in children

https://www.hsph.harvard.edu/news/features/fluoride-childrens-health-grandjean-choi/

Inferring the fluoride hydrogeochemistry and effect of consuming fluoride-contaminated drinking water on human health in some endemic areas of Birbhum district, West Bengal.

https://www.ncbi.nlm.nih.gov/pubmed/26164468

Intelligence quotient of 7 to 9 year-old children from an area with high fluoride in drinking water

http://www.academicjournals.org/article/article1379419220_P oureslami%20%20et%20al.pdf

Intelligence quotients of 12-14 year old school children in a high and a low fluoride village in india

https://www.researchgate.net/publication/287694642_Intellige nce_quotients_of_12-
14_year_old_school_children_in_a_high_and_a_low_fluoride_v illage_in_india

INVESTIGATION OF INTELLIGENCE QUOTIENT IN 9–12-YEAR-OLD CHILDREN EXPOSED TO HIGH- AND LOW-DRINKING WATER FLUORIDE IN WEST AZERBAIJAN PROVINCE, IRAN

http://www.fluorideresearch.org/471/files/FJ2014_v47_n1_p00 9-014_sfs.pdf

Modifying effect of COMT gene polymorphism and a predictive role for proteomics analysis in children's intelligence in endemic fluorosis area in Tianjin, China

https://www.ncbi.nlm.nih.gov/pubmed/25556215

Physiologic Conditions Affect Toxicity of Ingested Industrial Fluoride

https://www.ncbi.nlm.nih.gov/pmc/articles/PMC3690253/

Reducing Exposure to High Fluoride Drinking Water in Estonia— A Countrywide Study

https://www.ncbi.nlm.nih.gov/pmc/articles/PMC3987025/

Relationship Between Dental Fluorosis and Intelligence Quotient of School Going Children In and Around Lucknow District: A Cross-Sectional Study

http://www.jcdr.net/article_abstract.asp?issn=0973-709x&year=2015&month=November&volume=9&issue=11&page=ZC10-ZC15&id=6726

Relation between dental fluorosis and intelligence quotient in school children of Bagalkot district.

https://www.ncbi.nlm.nih.gov/pubmed/21911949

RESEARCH ON THE EFFECTS OF FLUORIDE ON CHILD INTELLECTUAL DEVELOPMENT UNDER DIFFERENT ENVIRONMENTAL CONDITIONS
http://www.fluorideresearch.org/412/files/FJ2008_v41_n2_p15 6-160.pdf

Risk Assessment of Fluoride Intake from Tea in the Republic of Ireland and its Implications for Public Health and Water Fluoridation

https://www.ncbi.nlm.nih.gov/pmc/articles/PMC4808922/

The effects of comprehensive control measures on intelligence of school-age children in coal-burning-borne endemic fluorosis areas

https://www.researchgate.net/publication/289863716_The_eff ects_of_comprehensive_control_measures_on_intelligence_of_ school-age_children_in_coal-burning-
borne_endemic_fluorosis_areas

The Effects of High Levels of Fluoride and Iodine on Child Intellectual Ability and the Metabolism of Fluoride and Iodine
https://www.researchgate.net/publication/237279822_The_Eff ects_of_High_Levels_of_Fluoride_and_Iodine_on_Child_Intellec tual_Ability_and_the_Metabolism_of_Fluoride_and_Iodine

The Effects of High Fluoride on the Intelligence Level of Primary and Secondary Students

http://www.fluoridealert.org/wp-content/uploads/an-1992.pdf
A preliminary investigation of the IQs of 7-13 year-old children from an area with coal burning-related fluoride poisoning
https://www.researchgate.net/publication/237283559 A preliminary investigation of the IQs of 7-13 year-old children from an area with coal burning-related fluoride poisoning

The relationships between low levels of urine fluoride on children's intelligence, dental fluorosis in endemic fluorosis areas in Hulunbuir, Inner Mongolia, China.

https://www.ncbi.nlm.nih.gov/pubmed/21237562

Water Fluoridation: A Critical Review of the Physiological Effects of Ingested Fluoride as a Public Health Intervention

https://www.ncbi.nlm.nih.gov/pmc/articles/PMC3956646/

Gardasil

Acute Disseminated Encephalomyelitis Following Immunization with Human Papillomavirus Vaccines

https://www.jstage.jst.go.jp/article/internalmedicine/55/21/55_55.7217/_article

Adolescent Premature Ovarian Insufficiency Following Human Papillomavirus Vaccination: A Case Series Seen in General Practice

https://www.ncbi.nlm.nih.gov/m/pubmed/26425627/

Adverse events following HPV vaccination, Alberta 2006-2014

https://www.ncbi.nlm.nih.gov/m/pubmed/26921782/

Association of acute cerebellar ataxia and human papilloma virus vaccination: a case report

https://www.ncbi.nlm.nih.gov/m/pubmed/23378179/

Autoimmune hepatitis type 2 following anti-papillomavirus vaccination in a 11-year-old girl

https://www.ncbi.nlm.nih.gov/m/pubmed/21596082/

Behavioral abnormalities in female mice following administration of aluminum adjuvants and the human papillomavirus (HPV) vaccine Gardasil

https://www.ncbi.nlm.nih.gov/m/pubmed/27421722/

Bivalent HPV vaccine safety depending on subtypes of juvenile idiopathic arthritis
http://ard.bmj.com/content/73/12/e75.long

Brachial plexus neuritis following HPV vaccination

https://www.ncbi.nlm.nih.gov/m/pubmed/18602437/

A case-control study of quadrivalent human papillomavirus vaccine-associated autoimmune adverse events

https://www.ncbi.nlm.nih.gov/m/pubmed/25535199/

CNS demyelination and quadrivalent HPV vaccination

https://www.ncbi.nlm.nih.gov/m/pubmed/18805844/

Demyelinating disease and polyvalent human papilloma virus vaccination
http://jnnp.bmj.com/content/82/11/1296.long

Demyelinating disease and vaccination of the human papillomavirus

https://www.ncbi.nlm.nih.gov/m/pubmed/21425100/

Development of unilateral cervical and supraclavicular lymphadenopathy after human papilloma virus vaccination

https://www.ncbi.nlm.nih.gov/m/pubmed/18752390/

Erythema multiforme following vaccination for human papillomavirus

https://www.ncbi.nlm.nih.gov/m/pubmed/19887766/

Fibromyalgia-Like Illness in 2 Girls After Human Papillomavirus Vaccination
http://journals.lww.com/jclinrheum/Citation/2014/10000/Fibro myalgia_Like_Illness_in_2_Girls_After_Human.12.aspx

HPV-negative Gastric Type Adenocarcinoma In Situ of the Cervix: A Spectrum of Rare Lesions Exhibiting Gastric and Intestinal Differentiation

http://insights.ovid.com/crossref?an=00000478-900000000-98079

HPV vaccination syndrome. A questionnaire-based study

https://www.ncbi.nlm.nih.gov/m/pubmed/26354426/

Human papilloma virus vaccine and primary ovarian failure: another facet of the autoimmune/inflammatory syndrome induced by adjuvants.

https://www.ncbi.nlm.nih.gov/m/pubmed/23902317/

Human papillomavirus (HPV) vaccines as an option for preventing cervical malignancies: (how) effective and safe?

https://www.ncbi.nlm.nih.gov/m/pubmed/23016780/

Human papillomavirus vaccine and systemic lupus erythematosus

https://www.ncbi.nlm.nih.gov/m/pubmed/23624585/

Human papilloma virus vaccine associated uveitis

https://www.ncbi.nlm.nih.gov/m/pubmed/24191906/

Human papillomavirus vaccines, complex regional pain syndrome, postural orthostatic tachycardia syndrome, and autonomic dysfunction - a review of the regulatory evidence from the European Medicines Agency

https://www.ncbi.nlm.nih.gov/m/pubmed/27867145/

Hypersensitivity reaction to human papillomavirus vaccine due to polysorbate 80

https://www.ncbi.nlm.nih.gov/m/pubmed/22605841/

Hypersensitivity reactions to human papillomavirus vaccine in Australian schoolgirls: retrospective cohort study

https://www.ncbi.nlm.nih.gov/m/pubmed/19050332/

Hypothesis: Human papillomavirus vaccination syndrome--small fiber neuropathy and dysautonomia could be its underlying pathogenesis

https://www.ncbi.nlm.nih.gov/m/pubmed/25990003/

Immune thrombocytopenic purpura following human papillomavirus vaccination

https://www.ncbi.nlm.nih.gov/m/pubmed/19464550/

Kikuchi-Fujimoto disease following vaccination against human papilloma virus infection and Japanese encephalitis

https://www.ncbi.nlm.nih.gov/m/pubmed/22476507/

Lichenoid Drug Eruption After Human Papillomavirus Vaccination

http://onlinelibrary.wiley.com/doi/10.1111/pde.12516/full

A link between human papilloma virus vaccination and primary ovarian insufficiency: current analysis

https://www.ncbi.nlm.nih.gov/m/pubmed/26125978/

Neurologic Complications in HPV Vaccination

https://www.ncbi.nlm.nih.gov/m/pubmed/26160812/

On the relationship between human papilloma virus vaccine and autoimmune diseases

https://www.ncbi.nlm.nih.gov/m/pubmed/24468416/

225

Orthostatic intolerance and postural tachycardia syndrome as suspected adverse effects of vaccination against human papilloma virus

https://www.ncbi.nlm.nih.gov/m/pubmed/25882168/

Pancreatitis after human papillomavirus vaccination: a matter of molecular mimicry

https://www.ncbi.nlm.nih.gov/m/pubmed/27421720/

Pancreatitis following human papillomavirus vaccination

https://www.mja.com.au/journal/2008/189/3/pancreatitis-following-human-papillomavirus-vaccination

Panuveitis With Exudative Retinal Detachments After Vaccination Against Human Papilloma Virus

https://www.ncbi.nlm.nih.gov/m/pubmed/26469238/

Peripheral sympathetic nerve dysfunction in adolescent Japanese girls following immunization with the human papillomavirus vaccine

https://www.ncbi.nlm.nih.gov/m/pubmed/25274229/

Pharmaceutical Companies' Role in State Vaccination Policymaking: The Case of Human Papillomavirus Vaccination

https://www.ncbi.nlm.nih.gov/pmc/articles/PMC3483914/

Orthostatic intolerance and postural tachycardia syndrome as suspected adverse effects of vaccination against human papilloma virus

https://www.ncbi.nlm.nih.gov/m/pubmed/25882168/

Postural tachycardia syndrome following human papillomavirus vaccination

https://www.ncbi.nlm.nih.gov/m/pubmed/24102827/

Potential cross-reactivity between HPV16 L1 protein and sudden death-associated antigens

https://www.ncbi.nlm.nih.gov/m/pubmed/21699023/

Premature ovarian failure 3 years after menarche in a 16-year-old girl following human papillomavirus vaccination

https://www.ncbi.nlm.nih.gov/m/pubmed/23035167/

Severe manifestations of autoimmune syndrome induced by adjuvants (Shoenfeld's syndrome).

https://www.ncbi.nlm.nih.gov/m/pubmed/27412294/

Severe somatoform and dysautonomic syndromes after HPV vaccination: case series and review of literature

https://www.ncbi.nlm.nih.gov/m/pubmed/27503625/

A 16-year-old girl with bilateral visual loss and left hemiparesis following an immunization against human papilloma virus

https://www.ncbi.nlm.nih.gov/m/pubmed/20189933/

Small Fiber Neuropathy Following Vaccination

https://www.ncbi.nlm.nih.gov/m/pubmed/27552388/

Syncope and seizures following human papillomavirus vaccination: a retrospective case series

https://www.ncbi.nlm.nih.gov/m/pubmed/21449862/

Telogen effluvium following bivalent human papillomavirus vaccine administration: a report of two cases

https://www.ncbi.nlm.nih.gov/m/pubmed/22584489/

Two Cases of Acute Disseminated Encephalomyelitis Following Vaccination Against Human Papilloma Virus

https://www.ncbi.nlm.nih.gov/pmc/articles/PMC5140871/

Two unclear cases of death. Can we still recommend HPV vaccination?].

https://www.ncbi.nlm.nih.gov/m/pubmed/18361151/

An unmasking phenomenon in an observational post-licensure safety study of adolescent girls and young women

https://www.ncbi.nlm.nih.gov/m/pubmed/22580356/

Vaccine-related serious adverse events might have been under-recognized in the pivotal HPV vaccine randomized trial

http://link.springer.com/article/10.1007%2Fs10067-017-3575-z

Gardasil has never been proven to prevent cervical cancer

http://articles.mercola.com/sites/articles/archive/2013/01/24/hpv-vaccine-averting-cancer-unproven.aspx

Lead developer of HPV vaccine comes clean

http://www.collective-evolution.com/2016/04/12/lead-developer-of-hpv-vaccines-comes-clean-to-warn-parents-young-girls/

Vaccines and pregnancy

Acute disseminated encephalomyelitis after tetanus vaccination of a pregnant woman in Senegal

https://www.ncbi.nlm.nih.gov/m/pubmed/22868743/

Are toxic biometals destroying your children's future?

https://www.ncbi.nlm.nih.gov/m/pubmed/19205900/

Birth defects among infants born to women who received anthrax vaccine in pregnancy.

https://www.ncbi.nlm.nih.gov/m/pubmed/18599489/

Comparison of VAERS fetal-loss reports during three consecutive influenza seasons

https://www.ncbi.nlm.nih.gov/pmc/articles/PMC3888271/

Depressive symptoms predict exaggerated inflammatory responses to an *in vivo* immune challenge among pregnant women

https://www.ncbi.nlm.nih.gov/pmc/articles/PMC2787729/

Diphtheria-tetanus-pertussis vaccine administered simultaneously with measles vaccine is associated with increased morbidity and poor growth in girls. A randomised trial from Guinea-Bissau.

https://www.ncbi.nlm.nih.gov/pubmed/21093496

Fetal damage after accidental polio vaccination of an immune mother.

https://www.ncbi.nlm.nih.gov/m/pubmed/6747944/

Fetal and Perinatal Mortality: United States, 2013

https://www.cdc.gov/nchs/data/nvsr/nvsr64/nvsr64_08.pdf

Fetal Deaths Outnumber Infant Deaths for First Time in US

http://www.medscape.com/viewarticle/848656

Guillain-Barré Syndrome after H1N1 Shot in Pregnancy: Maternal and Fetal Care in the Third Trimester—Case Report

https://www.ncbi.nlm.nih.gov/pmc/articles/PMC3521405/

Influenza Vaccination in the First Trimester of Pregnancy and Risk of Autism Spectrum Disorder

http://jamanetwork.com/journals/jamapediatrics/article-abstract/2617988

Inflammatory Responses to Trivalent Influenza Virus Vaccine Among Pregnant Women

https://www.ncbi.nlm.nih.gov/pmc/articles/PMC3204610/#!po=5.55556

Major Birth Defects after Vaccination Reported to the Vaccine Adverse Event Reporting System (VAERS), 1990 to 2014.

https://www.ncbi.nlm.nih.gov/m/pubmed/28398711/

Persistent fetal rubella vaccine virus infection following inadvertent vaccination during early pregnancy.

https://www.ncbi.nlm.nih.gov/m/pubmed/10745249/

Pregnancy and the immune system: between tolerance and rejection.

https://www.ncbi.nlm.nih.gov/pubmed/12581692

Vaccines, biotechnology and their connection with induced abortion

https://www.ncbi.nlm.nih.gov/m/pubmed/18611078/

Yellow fever vaccination during pregnancy and spontaneous abortion: a case-control study.

https://www.ncbi.nlm.nih.gov/m/pubmed/9484965/

Thimerosal

A dose-response relationship between organic mercury exposure from thimerosal-containing vaccines and neurodevelopmental disorders.

https://www.ncbi.nlm.nih.gov/pubmed/25198681

Abating Mercury Exposure in Young Children Should Include Thimerosal-Free Vaccines

https://www.ncbi.nlm.nih.gov/pubmed/28439753

Acute exposure to thimerosal induces antiproliferative properties, apoptosis, and autophagy activation in human Chang conjunctival cells

https://www.ncbi.nlm.nih.gov/pubmed/24384799

Activation of methionine synthase by insulin-like growth factor-1 and dopamine: a target for neurodevelopmental toxins and thimerosal.

https://www.ncbi.nlm.nih.gov/pubmed/14745455

Administration of Thimerosal to Infant Rats Increases Overflow of Glutamate and Aspartate in the Prefrontal Cortex: Protective Role of Dehydroepiandrosterone Sulfate https://www.ncbi.nlm.nih.gov/pmc/articles/PMC3264864/?tool=pubmed

Alkyl Mercury-Induced Toxicity: Multiple Mechanisms of Action

https://www.ncbi.nlm.nih.gov/pubmed/27161558

Alternatively Spliced Methionine Synthase in SH-SY5Y Neuroblastoma Cells: Cobalamin and GSH Dependence and Inhibitory Effects of Neurotoxic Metals and Thimerosal

https://www.ncbi.nlm.nih.gov/pubmed/26989453

An assessment of downward trends in neurodevelopmental disorders in the United States following removal of Thimerosal from childhood vaccines

https://www.ncbi.nlm.nih.gov/pubmed/16733480

A brain proteome profile in rats exposed to methylmercury or thimerosal (ethylmercury).

https://www.ncbi.nlm.nih.gov/pubmed/27294299

A bioethical j'accuse: analysis of the discussion around thiomersal in Chile

https://www.ncbi.nlm.nih.gov/pubmed/25197986

A systematic study of the disposition and metabolism of mercury species in mice after exposure to low levels of thimerosal (ethylmercury).

https://www.ncbi.nlm.nih.gov/pubmed/25173055

A meta-analysis of the evidence on the impact of prenatal and early infancy exposures to mercury on autism and attention deficit/hyperactivity disorder in the childhood

https://www.ncbi.nlm.nih.gov/pubmed/24952233

A review of Thimerosal (Merthiolate) and its ethylmercury breakdown product: specific historical considerations regarding safety and effectiveness

https://www.ncbi.nlm.nih.gov/pubmed/18049924

A two-phase study evaluating the relationship between Thimerosal-containing vaccine administration and the risk for an autism spectrum disorder diagnosis in the United States

https://www.ncbi.nlm.nih.gov/pubmed/24354891

Blood Levels of Mercury Are Related to Diagnosis of Autism: A Reanalysis of an Important Data Set

http://journals.sagepub.com/doi/abs/10.1177/0883073807307111

Brain and tissue levels of mercury after chronic methylmercury exposure in the monkey.

https://www.ncbi.nlm.nih.gov/pubmed/2499694

Comparison of Blood and Brain Mercury Levels in Infant Monkeys Exposed to Methylmercury or Vaccines Containing Thimerosal

https://www.ncbi.nlm.nih.gov/pmc/articles/PMC1280342/

Dose-response analysis indicating time-dependent neurotoxicity caused by organic and inorganic mercury-Implications for toxic effects in the developing brain

https://www.ncbi.nlm.nih.gov/pubmed/26945727

Dose-response study of thimerosal-induced murine systemic autoimmunity

https://www.ncbi.nlm.nih.gov/pubmed/14736497

Effects of thimerosal on NGF signal transduction and cell death in neuroblastoma cells

https://www.ncbi.nlm.nih.gov/pubmed/15843506

Effect of thimerosal, a preservative in vaccines, on intracellular Ca2+ concentration of rat cerebellar neurons

https://www.ncbi.nlm.nih.gov/pubmed/14698570

Effect of thimerosal on the neurodevelopment of premature rats.

https://www.ncbi.nlm.nih.gov/pubmed/24235069

Embryonic exposure to thimerosal, an organomercury compound, causes abnormal early development of serotonergic neurons

https://www.ncbi.nlm.nih.gov/pubmed/21669256

Ethylmercury and Hg2+ induce the formation of neutrophil extracellular traps (NETs) by human neutrophil granulocytes

https://www.ncbi.nlm.nih.gov/pubmed/25701957

Exposure to mercury during the first six months via human milk and vaccines: modifying risk factors

https://www.ncbi.nlm.nih.gov/pubmed/17564957

Evaluation of cytotoxicity attributed to thimerosal on murine and human kidney cells

https://www.ncbi.nlm.nih.gov/pubmed/18049999

Flow-cytometric analysis on cytotoxic effect of thimerosal, a preservative in vaccines, on lymphocytes dissociated from rat thymic glands

https://www.ncbi.nlm.nih.gov/pubmed/15649632

Gender-selective toxicity of thimerosal

https://www.ncbi.nlm.nih.gov/pubmed/18771903

Genotoxicity of thimerosal in cultured human lymphocytes with and without metabolic activation sister chromatid exchange analysis proliferation index and mitotic index

https://www.ncbi.nlm.nih.gov/pubmed/18321677

Iatrogenic exposure to mercury after hepatitis B vaccination in preterm infants

http://www.sciencedirect.com/science/article/pii/S0022347600896560

Inhibition of the human thioredoxin system. A molecular mechanism of mercury toxicity.

https://www.ncbi.nlm.nih.gov/pubmed/18321861

In vitro study of thimerosal reactions in human whole blood and plasma surrogate samples

https://www.ncbi.nlm.nih.gov/pubmed/24613139

Intermingled modulatory and neurotoxic effects of thimerosal and mercuric ions on electrophysiological responses to GABA and NMDA in hippocampal neurons

https://www.ncbi.nlm.nih.gov/pubmed/21224507

Induction of metallothionein in mouse cerebellum and cerebrum with low-dose thimerosal injection

https://www.ncbi.nlm.nih.gov/pubmed/19357975

Integrating experimental (in vitro and in vivo) neurotoxicity studies of low-dose thimerosal relevant to vaccines.

https://www.ncbi.nlm.nih.gov/pubmed/21350943

Lasting neuropathological changes in rat brain after intermittent neonatal administration of thimerosal

https://www.ncbi.nlm.nih.gov/pubmed/21225508

Low-dose mercury exposure in early life: relevance of thimerosal to fetuses, newborns and infants

https://www.ncbi.nlm.nih.gov/pubmed/23992327

Making sense of epidemiological studies of young children exposed to thimerosal in vaccines

https://www.ncbi.nlm.nih.gov/pubmed/20638374

Maternal thimerosal exposure results in aberrant cerebellar oxidative stress, thyroid hormone metabolism, and motor behavior in rat pups; sex- and strain-dependent effects.

https://www.ncbi.nlm.nih.gov/pubmed/22015705

Mechanisms of Hg species induced toxicity in cultured human astrocytes: genotoxicity and DNA-damage response

https://www.ncbi.nlm.nih.gov/pubmed/24549367

Mercury induces inflammatory mediator release from human mast cells

http://download.springer.com/static/pdf/85/art%253A10.1186%252F1742-2094-7-20.pdf?originUrl=http%3A%2F%2Fjneuroinflammation.biomedcentral.com%2Farticle%2F10.1186%2F1742-2094-7-20&token2=exp=1496186083~acl=%2Fstatic%2Fpdf%2F85%2Fa

rt%25253A10.1186%25252F1742-2094-7-20.pdf*~hmac=1a606e4ed692efa79fd0271961676e30fef08e01
9899f3fe470e5f988353e82f

Mercury levels and human health in the Amazon Basin

https://www.ncbi.nlm.nih.gov/pubmed/27230737

Mercury toxicity and neurodegenerative effects

https://www.ncbi.nlm.nih.gov/pubmed/24515807

Mercury toxicokinetics--dependency on strain and gender

https://www.ncbi.nlm.nih.gov/pubmed/19732784

Mercury toxicity: Genetic susceptibility and synergistic effects

http://www.1796kotok.com/pdfs/haley.pdf

Methodological issues and evidence of malfeasance in research purporting to show thimerosal in vaccines is safe.

https://www.ncbi.nlm.nih.gov/pubmed/24995277

Mitochondrial dysfunction, impaired oxidative-reduction activity, degeneration, and death in human neuronal and fetal cells induced by low-level exposure to thimerosal and other metal compounds

https://www.ncbi.nlm.nih.gov/pubmed/24532866

Modeling neurodevelopment outcomes and ethylmercury exposure from thimerosal-containing vaccines

https://www.ncbi.nlm.nih.gov/pubmed/18364366

Neonatal administration of a vaccine preservative, thimerosal, produces lasting impairment of nociception and apparent activation of opioid system in rats.

https://www.ncbi.nlm.nih.gov/pubmed/19747466?itool=Entrez System2.PEntrez.Pubmed.Pubmed_ResultsPanel.Pubmed_RVDo cSum&ordinalpos=1

Persistent behavioral impairments and alterations of brain dopamine system after early postnatal administration of thimerosal in rats

https://www.ncbi.nlm.nih.gov/pubmed/21549155

Sensitization effect of thimerosal is mediated in vitro via reactive oxygen species and calcium signaling

http://www.sciencedirect.com/science/article/pii/S0300483X10 002040

Suppression by thimerosal of ex-vivo CD4+ T cell response to influenza vaccine and induction of apoptosis in primary memory T cells

https://www.ncbi.nlm.nih.gov/pubmed/24690681

The retention time of inorganic mercury in the brain — A systematic review of the evidence

http://www.sciencedirect.com/science/article/pii/S0041008X13 005644

Thimerosal-Derived Ethylmercury Is a Mitochondrial Toxin in Human Astrocytes: Possible Role of Fenton Chemistry in the Oxidation and Breakage of mtDNA

https://www.ncbi.nlm.nih.gov/pmc/articles/PMC3395253/

Thimerosal induces apoptotic and fibrotic changes to kidney epithelial cells in vitro

https://www.ncbi.nlm.nih.gov/pubmed/24942245

Thimerosal-induced apoptosis in mouse C2C12 myoblast cells occurs through suppression of the PI3K/Akt/survivin pathway

https://www.ncbi.nlm.nih.gov/pubmed/23145070

Thimerosal exposure & increasing trends of premature puberty in the vaccine safety datalink

https://www.ncbi.nlm.nih.gov/pubmed/20424300

Thimerosal exposure in infants and neurodevelopmental disorders: an assessment of computerized medical records in the Vaccine Safety Datalink.

https://www.ncbi.nlm.nih.gov/pubmed/18482737

Thimerosal-induced limbal stem cell failure: report of a case and review of the literature

https://www.ncbi.nlm.nih.gov/pubmed/17630628

Thimerosal-induced cytosolic Ca2+ elevation and subsequent cell death in human osteosarcoma cells

https://www.ncbi.nlm.nih.gov/pubmed/15964764

Thimerosal induces DNA breaks, caspase-3 activation, membrane damage, and cell death in cultured human neurons and fibroblasts

https://www.ncbi.nlm.nih.gov/pubmed/12773768

Thimerosal induces micronuclei in the cytochalasin B block micronucleus test with human lymphocytes

https://www.ncbi.nlm.nih.gov/pubmed/12491041

Thimerosal neurotoxicity is associated with glutathione depletion: protection with glutathione precursors

https://www.ncbi.nlm.nih.gov/pubmed/15527868

Thimerosal distribution and metabolism in neonatal mice: comparison with methyl mercury

https://www.ncbi.nlm.nih.gov/pubmed/17582588

Thimerosal induces oxidative stress in HeLa S epithelial cells

https://www.ncbi.nlm.nih.gov/pubmed/21783709

Thimerosal induces toxic reactions.

https://www.ncbi.nlm.nih.gov/pubmed/7981614

Thimerosal induces toxic reaction in non-sensitized animals.

https://www.ncbi.nlm.nih.gov/pubmed/7518269

Thiomersal as a vaccine preservative.

https://www.ncbi.nlm.nih.gov/pubmed/10697462

Transcriptomic analyses of neurotoxic effects in mouse brain after intermittent neonatal administration of thimerosal.

https://www.ncbi.nlm.nih.gov/pubmed/24675092

Toxicity of ethylmercury (and Thimerosal): a comparison with methylmercury

https://www.ncbi.nlm.nih.gov/pubmed/23401210

Toxicity of organic and inorganic mercury species in differentiated human neurons and human astrocytes

https://www.ncbi.nlm.nih.gov/pubmed/26302930

Toxicological effects of thiomersal and ethylmercury: Inhibition of the thioredoxin system and NADP(+)-dependent dehydrogenases of the pentose phosphate pathway

https://www.ncbi.nlm.nih.gov/pubmed/25981166

Transcriptomic analyses of neurotoxic effects in mouse brain after intermittent neonatal administration of thimerosal

https://www.ncbi.nlm.nih.gov/pubmed/24675092

Uncoupling of ATP-Mediated Calcium Signaling and Dysregulated Interleukin-6 Secretion in Dendritic Cells by Nanomolar Thimerosal

https://www.ncbi.nlm.nih.gov/pmc/articles/PMC1513334/

Vaccines without thiomersal: why so necessary, why so long coming?

https://www.ncbi.nlm.nih.gov/pubmed/11368282

"Intentional subcutaneous or intravenous injection of elemental mercury results in toxicity similar to chronic inorganic mercury exposure, but can also result in severe tissue damage that may require extensive surgical debridement. On the contrary, ingestion of elemental mercury is generally benign and as there is almost no absorption of this form from the GI tract. "
http://www.calpoison.org/hcp/2011/callusvol9no1.htm

These findings document neurotoxic effects of thimerosal, at doses equivalent to those used in infant vaccines or higher, in developing rat brain, suggesting likely involvement of this mercurial in neurodevelopmental disorders."
http://www.ncbi.nlm.nih.gov/pubmed/21225508

Data demonstrated that Hg exposures, particularly during the first trimester of pregnancy, at well-established dose/weight ratios produced severe damage to humans including death. . In light of research suggestive of a mercuric risk factor for childhood conditions such as tic disorders, cerebral palsy, and autism, it is essential that Hg advisories account for secondary

prenatal human exposures."
http://www.tandfonline.com/.../f.../10.1080/02772248.2012.72
4574

" High blood mercury level was associated with ADHD. Whether
the relationship is causal requires further studies."
http://www.ncbi.nlm.nih.gov/pubmed/?term=17177150

The stubborn insistence of some vaccine manufacturers and
health agencies on continuation of use of this proven
neurotoxin in vaccines is testimony of their disregard for both
the health of young generations and for the environment.*
http://www.ncbi.nlm.nih.gov/pubmed/22015977

We propose that children with the autism diagnosis are
especially vulnerable to toxic metals such as aluminum and
mercury due to insufficient serum sulfate and glutathione. A
strong correlation between autism and the MMR (Measles,
Mumps, Rubella) vaccine is also observed, which may be
partially explained via an increased sensitivity to
acetaminophen administered to control fever."
http://www.mdpi.com/1099-4300/14/11/2227
full text: http://groups.csail.mit.edu/.../pub.../2012/entropy-14-
02227.pdf

Thimerosal, an organomercurial added as a preservative to
some vaccines, is a suspected iatrogenic factor, possibly
contributing to paediatric neurodevelopmental disorders
including autism. We examined the effects of early postnatal
administration of thimerosal (four i.m. injections, 12 or 240 µg
THIM-Hg/kg, on postnatal days 7, 9, 11 and 15) on brain
pathology in Wistar rats. Numerous neuropathological changes
were observed in young adult rats which were treated
postnatally with thimerosal. They included: ischaemic
degeneration of neurons and "dark" neurons in the prefrontal
and temporal cortex, the hippocampus and the cerebellum,
pathological changes of the blood vessels in the temporal
cortex, diminished synaptophysin reaction in the hippocampus,
atrophy of astroglia in the hippocampus and cerebellum, and
positive caspase-3 reaction in Bergmann astroglia. These

findings document neurotoxic effects of thimerosal, at doses equivalent to those used in infant vaccines or higher, in developing rat brain, suggesting likely involvement of this mercurial in neurodevelopmental disorders.
http://www.ncbi.nlm.nih.gov/pubmed/21225508

"We find that ethylmercury not only inhibits mitochondrial respiration leading to a drop in the steady state membrane potential, but also concurrent with these phenomena increases the formation of superoxide, hydrogen peroxide, and Fenton/Haber-Weiss generated hydroxyl radical. These oxidants increase the levels of cellular aldehyde/ketones. Additionally, we find a five-fold increase in the levels of oxidant damaged mitochondrial DNA bases and increases in the levels of mtDNA nicks and blunt-ended breaks.. These mitochondria appear to have undergone a permeability transition, an observation supported by the five-fold increase in Caspase-3 activity observed after Thimerosal treatment."
*the next time someone says that ethylmercury is ok for children ask them to read this article.
http://www.ncbi.nlm.nih.gov/pmc/articles/PMC3395253/

"An average-sized pregnant woman receiving an influenza vaccine will be exposed to organic mercury that exceeds the EPA limit by a factor of 3.5 (Table 4). The fetus could potentially receive a dose of mercury that exceeds EPAlimits by a much larger factor. Furthermore, fetal blood mercury concentrations have been shown to be as much as 4.3 times the maternal level. Alarger proportion of ethyl mercury accumulates in fetal tissues relative to maternal tissues, especially in the central nervous system. The observation of a 7.8-15.7% prevalence of elevated umbilical cord mercury in the United States, at levels associated with loss of IQ, adds to the significance of additional mercury exposure from prenatal vaccination.
http://www.jpands.org/vol11no2/ayoub.pdf

Administration of thimerosal to infant rats increases overflow of glutamate and aspartate in the prefrontal cortex: protective role of dehydroepiandrosterone sulfate. Neurochem Res. 2012

Comparison of Blood and Brain Mercury Levels in Infant Monkeys Exposed to Methylmercury or Vaccines Containing Thimerosal. Environmental Health Perspectives, August 2005
http://www.ncbi.nlm.nih.gov/pubmed/16079072

Integrating experimental (in vitro and in vivo) neurotoxicity studies of low-dose thimerosal relevant to vaccines. Neurochem Res. 2011
http://www.ncbi.nlm.nih.gov/pubmed/21350943

Lasting neuropathological changes in rat brain after intermittent neonatal administration of thimerosal. Folia Neuropathology, 2010
http://www.ncbi.nlm.nih.gov/pubmed/21225508

Maternal thimerosal exposure results in aberrant cerebellar oxidative stress, thyroid hormone metabolism, and motor behavior in rat pups; sex and strain dependent effects. Cerebellum. 2012
http://www.ncbi.nlm.nih.gov/pubmed/22015705

Neonatal administration of thimerosal causes persistent changes in mu opioid receptors in the rat brain. Neurochem Res. 2010
http://www.ncbi.nlm.nih.gov/pubmed/20803069

Neurodevelopmental disorders following thimerosal containing childhood immunizations: a followup analysis International Journal of Toxicology, 2004
http://www.ncbi.nlm.nih.gov/pubmed/15764492

Persistent behavioral impairments and alterations of brain dopamine system after early postnatal administration of thimerosal in rats. Behav Brain Res, 2011
http://www.ncbi.nlm.nih.gov/pubmed/21549155

Thimerosal induces neuronal cell apoptosis by causing cytochrome c and apoptosisinducing factor release from mitochondria. International Journal of Molecular Medicine, 2006

Thimerosal Exposure and the Role of Sulfation Chemistry and Thiol Availability in Autism Int. J. Environ. Res. Public Health 2013
www.mdpi.com/journal/ijerph

If you would like to get in touch with the authors, contact us at

info@soyouregoingtohaveababy.com

We'd be glad to help in any way we can.

However – we are not doctors. So don't ask us medical questions. We cannot – and will not – give medical advice.

We will probably ask you to just use some common-sense judgment however.

So please don't waste your time – or ours – asking us to do something that is not what we are here to do.

That's why there are doctors – bring your medical questions to them.

That's what they are paid (and trained) to do.

We gladly however welcome information in the form of corrections or pointing out possible mistakes – and absolutely welcome people to share more studies that they think would be helpful to be included in later versions of the book. We did not have time to hunt down every single one – but that also wasn't our goal. Our goal was more so to bring awareness to the questions that should be asked – vs providing a million different studies and telling you what to do. The studies in the book are just to prove that there are studies that exist that question the narrative that we have been told. We eventually plan to have an extremely extensive list available at www.soyouregoingtohaveababy.com when we get the time.

Finally we have a few books that we highly recommend if you would like to delve deeper into the "other side" of vaccine safety.

Dissolving Illusions: Suzanne Humphries MD
http://amzn.to/2ryudwQ

Miller's Review of Critical Vaccine Studies: 400 Important Scientific Papers Summarized for Parents and Researchers
http://amzn.to/2taukvR

The Vaccine-Friendly Plan: Dr. Paul's Safe and Effective Approach to Immunity and Health-from Pregnancy Through Your Child's Teen Years
http://amzn.to/2tahZaW

What Your Doctor May Not Tell You About(TM) Children's Vaccinations
http://amzn.to/2sAlvNk

Vaccine Epidemic: How Corporate Greed, Biased Science, and Coercive Government Threaten Our Human Rights, Our Health, and Our Children
http://amzn.to/2rnugra

The Environmental and Genetic Causes of Autism: James Lyons-Weiler PHD
http://amzn.to/2ro0QJg

VACCINE PRIMER: AN INOCULATION

http://vaccineprimer.weebly.com/the-author.html

Plague: One Scientist's Intrepid Search for the Truth about Human Retroviruses and Chronic Fatigue Syndrome (ME/CFS), Autism, and Other Diseases caused by vaccine contamination
http://amzn.to/2FWwyp3

Crooked: Man-Made Disease Explained: The incredible story of metal, microbes, and medicine - hidden within our faces.
(THIS BOOK IS AWESOME!!!!!)
http://amzn.to/2FWZJIV

You MAY ALSO CHECK OUT MY PERSONAL PAGE AT:

WWW.STAYHEALTHYMYFRIENDS.WIN

FOR THE LATEST SUPPLEMENTS, ESSENTIAL OIL
INFORMATION, RESEARCH TOPICS, EPIGENETICS
UPDATES, AND JUST PLAIN INTERESTING
INFORMATION FROM AROUND THE WORLD

IF YOU OR A LOVED ONE HAS A STORY TO SHARE
REGARDING ANY MEDICAL PROCEDURE OR
PRODUCT – HEAD OVER TO THE FORUM AT
WWW.SOYOUREGOINGTOHAVEABABY.COM AND
SHARE IT WITH PEOPLE. IT'S ALL ABOUT PARENTS
HELPING PARENTS.

~Adam Ringham

Printed in Great Britain
by Amazon

44441474R00142